A Personal Guide to the Tax Cuts and Jobs Act:

What It Means For You

By Susan Flax Posner

Wolters Kluwer

ISBN: 978-0-8080-4968-5

Contents

Highlights of the Act

Highlights of the Tax Cuts and Jobs Act Pertaining to Individuals

The "Tax Cuts and Jobs Act" is the largest piece of major tax reform legislation to be enacted in over three decades. The new law was approved by Congress on December 20, 2017 and signed into law by the President on December 22, 2017. The Act has an official title, but it has been represented in popular media as the "Tax Cuts and Jobs Act," and will be referred to as that throughout this book.

This new sweeping tax law would affect individuals and businesses in dramatic ways, generally for eight years beginning on January 1, 2018 and through December 31, 2025, when many of the provisions of the law are scheduled to sunset or expire.

Major Tax Changes Made by Tax Cuts and Jobs Act

The major tax changes made by the Tax Cuts and Jobs Act are highlighted below:

New Income Tax Rates and Brackets. The Tax Cuts and Jobs Act temporarily changes the structure of the individual income tax by modifying the rate structure. Beginning on January 1, 2018 and until December 31, 2025, the new tax brackets will be 10%, 12%, 22%, 24%, 32%, 35% and 37%.

Standard Deduction Increased. The size of the standard deduction is increased beginning on January 1, 2018 until December 31, 2025, so that in 2018 the standard deduction is $24,000 for joint filers, $18,000 for heads of household and $12,000 for other filers. There were no changes made to the standard deduction for the elderly and the blind.

Personal Exemptions Suspended. In another dramatic change, the new law temporarily eliminates an individual's deduction for personal exemptions. This change, like others, is effective January 1, 2018 and will sunset after December 31, 2025.

Kiddie Tax Revised. For the eight-year period beginning on January 1, 2018 and before January 1, 2026, the taxable income of a child attributable to earned income is taxed under the rates for single individuals and the taxable income of a child attributable to net unearned income (income from investments) is taxed according to the brackets applicable to estates and trusts (rather than the rates of the child's parents).

Child Tax Credit Increased. Beginning January 1, 2018, the Tax Cuts and Jobs Act temporarily increases the value of the child tax credit to $2,000, providing that no more than $1,400 per child will be refundable. This $1,400 limitation is indexed for inflation. To qualify for the child tax credit, a Social Security number must be provided for the qualifying child for whom such credit is claimed. These changes will expire on December 31, 2025.

State and Local Income Tax Deduction Suspended. Another change receiving a great deal of attention revolves around the temporary suspension of an individual's deduction for state and local income taxes. Beginning on January 1, 2018, individuals will only be able to deduct state, local, and foreign property taxes and state and local sales taxes if these taxes are paid in connection with carrying on a trade or business, or when related to expenses for the production of income. Under these new provisions, a taxpayer may claim an itemized deduction of up to $10,000 ($5,000 for a married taxpayer filing a separate return) for the aggregate of (1) state and local property taxes not paid or accrued in carrying on a trade or business, or other specified activity, and (2) state and local income, war profits, and excess profits taxes (or sales taxes in lieu of income, etc. taxes) paid or accrued in the taxable year. Foreign real property taxes may not be deducted under this exception.

Mortgage and Home Equity Indebtedness Interest Deduction Limited. For the eight tax years beginning after December 31, 2017 and before January 1, 2026, the deduction for interest on home equity indebtedness is suspended, and the deduction for mortgage interest is limited to underlying indebtedness of up to $750,000 ($375,000 for married taxpayers filing separately). For tax years after December 31, 2025, the prior $1 million/$500,000 limitations are restored and a taxpayer may treat up to these amounts as acquisition indebtedness regardless of when the indebtedness was incurred. The suspension for home equity indebtedness also ends for tax years beginning after December 31, 2025.

The new lower limit doesn't apply to any acquisition indebtedness incurred before December 15, 2017.

A taxpayer who has entered into a binding written contract before December 15, 2017 to close on the purchase of a principal residence before January 1, 2018, and who purchases such residence before April 1, 2018, shall be considered to incur acquisition indebtedness prior to December 15, 2017.

The $1 million/$500,000 limitations continue to apply to taxpayers who refinance existing qualified residence indebtedness that was incurred before December 15, 2017, so long as the indebtedness resulting from the refinancing doesn't exceed the amount of the refinanced indebtedness.

Medical Expense Deduction Threshold Temporarily Reduced. For tax years beginning after December 31, 2016 and ending before January 1, 2019, the threshold on medical expense deductions is reduced to 7.5 percent for all taxpayers. In addition, the rule limiting the medical expense deduction for AMT purposes to 10 percent of AGI doesn't apply to tax years beginning after December 31, 2016 and ending before January 1, 2019.

Charitable Contribution Deduction Limitation Increased. For contributions made in the eight tax years beginning after December 31, 2017 and before January 1, 2026, the 50 percent limitation for cash contributions to public charities and certain private foundations is increased to 60 percent. Contributions exceeding the 60-percent limitation are generally allowed to be carried forward and deducted for up to five years, subject to the later year's ceiling.

For contributions made in tax years beginning after December 31, 2016, the donee-reporting exemption from the contemporaneous written acknowledgment requirement is repealed.

Alimony Deduction by Payor/Inclusion by Payee Suspended. For any divorce or separation agreement executed after December 31, 2018, or executed before that date but modified after it (if the modification expressly provides that the new amendments apply), alimony and separate maintenance payments are not deductible by the payor-spouse and are not included in the income of the payee-spouse. Instead, income used for alimony is taxed at the rates applicable to the payor-spouse.

Miscellaneous Itemized Deductions Suspended. For the eight tax years beginning after December 31, 2017 and before January 1, 2026, the deduction for miscellaneous itemized deductions that are subject to the 2-percent floor is suspended.

Overall Limitation ("Pease" Limitation) on Itemized Deductions Suspended. For the eight tax years beginning after December 31, 2017 and before January 1, 2026, the "Pease limitation" on itemized deductions is suspended.

Exclusion for Moving Expense Reimbursements Suspended. For the eight tax years beginning after December 31, 2017 and before January 1, 2026, the exclusion for qualified moving expense reimbursements is suspended, except for members of the Armed Forces on active duty (and their spouses and dependents) who move pursuant to a military order and incident to a permanent change of station.

Moving Expenses Deduction Suspended. For the eight tax years beginning after December 31, 2017 and before January 1, 2026, the deduction for moving expenses is suspended, except for members of the Armed Forces on active duty who move pursuant to a military order and incident to a permanent change of station.

Deduction for Personal Casualty & Theft Losses Suspended. For the eight tax years beginning after December 31, 2017 and before January 1, 2026, the personal casualty and theft loss deduction is suspended, except for personal casualty losses incurred in a federally-declared disaster. However, where a taxpayer has personal casualty gains, the loss suspension doesn't apply to the extent that such loss does not exceed the gain.

Gambling Loss Limitation Modified. For the eight tax years beginning after December 31, 2017 and before January 1, 2026, the limitation on wagering losses is modified to provide that *all* deductions for expenses incurred in carrying out wagering transactions, and not just gambling losses, are limited to the extent of gambling winnings.

Carried Interest—New Holding Period Requirement. Effective for tax years beginning after December 31, 2017, a three-year holding period requirement is imposed in order for certain partnership interests received in connection with the performance of services to be taxed as long-term capital gain. If the three-year holding period is not met with respect to an applicable partnership interest held by the taxpayer, the taxpayer's gain will be treated as a short-term gain and will be taxed at ordinary income rates

New Tax Treatment of Pass-Through Business Income. A major change is made by the Tax Cuts and Jobs Act to the way that business income generated by pass-through entities such as limited liability companies (LLCs), partnerships, S corporations or sole proprietorships is taxed. Under the old law, the net income of these pass-through entities was not taxed at the entity level but was taxed instead by the owners of the business at their individual tax rate. Under the new law, for the eight tax years beginning after December 31, 2017 and before January 1, 2026, the Tax Cuts and Jobs Act adds a new section which provides that a non-corporate taxpayer, including a trust or estate, who has qualified business income (QBI) from a partnership, S corporation, or sole proprietorship may deduct:

(1) the *lesser* of: (a) the "combined qualified business income amount" of the taxpayer, or (b) 20% of the excess, if any, of the taxable income of the taxpayer for the tax year over the sum of net capital gain and the aggregate amount of the qualified cooperative dividends of the taxpayer for the tax year; *plus*

(2) the *lesser* of: (i) 20% of the aggregate amount of the qualified cooperative dividends of the taxpayer for the tax year, or (ii) taxable income (reduced by the net capital gain) of the taxpayer for the tax year.

The term "combined qualified business income amount" means, for any tax year, an amount equal to: (i) the deductible amount for each qualified trade or business of the taxpayer (defined as 20% of the taxpayer's QBI subject to the W-2 wage limitation); *plus* (ii) 20% of the aggregate amount of qualified real estate investment trust (REIT) dividends and qualified publicly traded partnership income of the taxpayer for the tax year.

QBI is generally defined as the net amount of "qualified items of income, gain, deduction, and loss" relating to any qualified trade or business of the taxpayer. For this purpose, qualified items of income, gain, deduction, and loss are items of income, gain, deduction, and loss to the extent these items are effectively connected with the conduct of a trade or business within the United States and included or allowed in determining taxable income for the year. If the net amount of qualified income, gain, deduction, and loss relating to qualified trade or businesses of the taxpayer for any tax year is less than zero, the amount is treated as a loss from a qualified trade or business in the succeeding tax year. QBI does *not* include: certain investment items; reasonable compensation paid to the taxpayer by any qualified trade or business for services rendered with respect to the trade or business; any guaranteed payment to a partner for services to the business; or a payment to a partner for services rendered with respect to the trade or business.

The 20% deduction is not allowed in computing adjusted gross income (AGI), but rather is allowed as a deduction reducing *taxable* income.

Limitations. A qualified trade or business's deductible amount generally cannot exceed the greater of:

(1) 50% of the W-2 wages with respect to the qualified trade or business, or
(2) the sum of 25% of the W-2 wages paid with respect to the qualified trade or business plus 2.5% of the unadjusted basis, immediately after acquisition, of all "qualified property." Qualified property is defined as tangible, depreciable property which is held by and available for use in the qualified trade or business at the close of the tax year, which is used at any point during the tax year in the production of qualified business income, the depreciable period for which has not ended before the close of the tax year.

For a partnership or S corporation, each partner or shareholder is treated as having W-2 wages and unadjusted basis for the tax year in an amount equal to his or her allocable share of the W-2 wages and unadjusted basis of the entity for the tax year. A partner's or shareholder's allocable share of W-2 wages is determined in the same way as the partner's or shareholder's allocable share of wage expenses. A partner's or shareholder's allocable share of the unadjusted basis of qualified property is determined in the same manner as the partner's or shareholder's allocable share of depreciation. For an S corporation, an allocable share is the shareholder's pro rata share of an item. However, the W-2 wages/qualified property limit does not apply if the taxpayer's taxable income for the tax year is equal to or less than $315,000 for married individuals filing jointly ($157,500 for other individuals). The application of the W-2 wage/qualified property limit is phased in for individuals with taxable income exceeding these thresholds, over the next $100,000 of taxable income for married individuals filing jointly ($50,000 for other individuals).

The new deduction does not apply to specified service businesses (excluding engineering and architecture) and trades or businesses that involve the performance of services that consist of investment-type activities. However, the service business limitation is phased in in the case of a taxpayer whose taxable income exceeds $315,000 for married individuals filing jointly ($157,500 for other individuals), both indexed for inflation after 2018. The benefit of the deduction for service businesses is phased out over the next $100,000 of taxable income for joint filers ($50,000 for other individuals).

The deduction also does not apply to the trade or business of being an employee.

The new deduction for pass-through income is also available to specified agricultural or horticultural cooperatives, in an amount equal to the lesser of (i) 20% of the excess of the co-op's gross income over any qualified cooperative dividends paid during the tax year for the tax year, or (ii) the greater of (a) 50% of the W-2 wages of the co-op with respect to its trade or business, or (b) the sum of 25% of the W-2 wages of the cooperative with respect to its trade or business plus 2.5% of the unadjusted basis immediately after acquisition of qualified property of the cooperative.

Individual Mandate Imposed by Affordable Care Act Repealed. Another dramatic change made by the Tax Cuts and Jobs Act is the repeal of the individual mandate under the Affordable Care Act (also known as Obamacare). This mandate required individuals to be covered by a health plan that provided at least minimum essential coverage or be subject to a penalty for failure to maintain the coverage (commonly referred to as the "individual mandate"). Minimum essential coverage includes government-sponsored programs (including Medicare, Medicaid, and CHIP, among others), eligible employer-sponsored plans, plans in the individual market, grandfathered group health plans and grandfathered health insurance coverage, and other coverage as recognized by the Secretary of Health and Human Services ("HHS") in coordination with the Secretary of the Treasury. The penalty tax was imposed for any month that an individual did not have minimum essential coverage unless the individual qualified for an exemption.

Estate and Gift Tax Retained but Exemption Amount Doubled. For estates of decedents dying and gifts made during the eight years after December 31, 2017 and before January 1, 2026, the Tax Cuts and Jobs Act doubles the base estate and gift tax exemption amount from $5 million to $10 million. The $10 million amount is indexed for inflation occurring after 2011 and is estimated to be approximately $11.2 million in 2018 ($22.4 million per married couple). The generation-skipping transfer tax exemption is also doubled. The maximum federal estate tax rate of 40 percent under current law is retained. As a result of the new doubled exclusion amounts, married couples dying in 2018 will be able to exempt up to an estimated $22.4 million from any federal estate or gift tax. However, anyone inheriting assets will continue to receive a stepped-up, date of death basis for those assets for purposes of any subsequent sale.

AMT Retained, with Higher Exemption Amounts. For the eight tax years beginning after December 31, 2017 and before January 1, 2026, the Tax Cuts and Jobs Act increases the AMT exemption amounts for individuals as follows:

- For joint returns and surviving spouses to $109,400;
- For single taxpayers to $70,300;
- For marrieds filing separately to $54,700.

Under the new law, the above exemption amounts are reduced (not below zero) to an amount equal to 25 percent of the amount by which the alternative taxable income of the taxpayer exceeds the phase-out amounts, increased as follows:

- For joint returns and surviving spouses to $1 million;
- For all other taxpayers (other than estates and trusts) to $500,000.

No changes were made to the AMT exemptions available to trusts and estates.

Comparison of Tax Cuts and Jobs Act (H.R. 1) and Prior Law

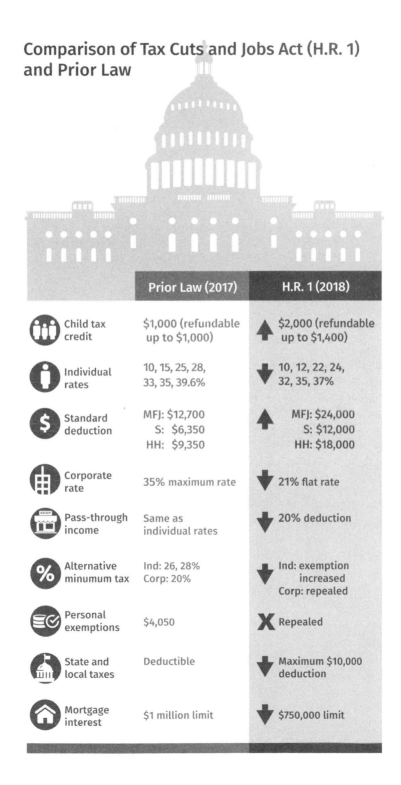

	Prior Law (2017)	H.R. 1 (2018)
Child tax credit	$1,000 (refundable up to $1,000)	$2,000 (refundable up to $1,400)
Individual rates	10, 15, 25, 28, 33, 35, 39.6%	10, 12, 22, 24, 32, 35, 37%
Standard deduction	MFJ: $12,700 S: $6,350 HH: $9,350	MFJ: $24,000 S: $12,000 HH: $18,000
Corporate rate	35% maximum rate	21% flat rate
Pass-through income	Same as individual rates	20% deduction
Alternative minumum tax	Ind: 26, 28% Corp: 20%	Ind: exemption increased Corp: repealed
Personal exemptions	$4,050	Repealed
State and local taxes	Deductible	Maximum $10,000 deduction
Mortgage interest	$1 million limit	$750,000 limit

CHAPTER 1

General Provisions Affecting Individuals

§ 1.01 Income Tax Rates of Individuals, Estates and Trusts

When an individual taxpayer determines regular tax liability, the individual generally must compute his or her taxable income and then apply the appropriate tax rate based on the tax rate schedule or the tax tables, if his or her taxable income is less than $100,000. The rate schedules are broken into several ranges of income, known as income brackets, and the marginal tax rate increases as a taxpayer's income increases. The Code provides four tax rate schedules for individuals based on filing status—*i.e.,* single, married filing jointly/surviving spouse, married filing separately, and head of household—each of which is divided into income ranges which are taxed at progressively higher marginal tax rates as income increases.

Under pre-Act law, individuals were subject to the following seven tax brackets: 10%, 15%, 25%, 28%, 33%, 35%, and 39.6%.

The new law provides that beginning on January 1, 2018 and before January 1, 2026, the following seven tax brackets will apply for individuals: 10%, 12%, 22%, 24%, 32%, 35% and 37%.

The new law also provides four tax brackets for estates and trusts: 10%, 24%, 35%, and 37%.

Tax Rate Schedules

Single

If taxable income is:	Then income tax equals:
Not over $9,525	10% of the taxable income
Over $9,525 but not over $38,700	$952.50 plus 12% of the excess over $9,525
Over $38,700 but not over $82,500	$4,453.50 plus 22% of the excess over $38,700
Over $82,500 but not over $157,500	$14,089.50 plus 24% of the excess over $82,500
Over $157,500 but not over $200,000	$32,089.50 plus 32% of the excess over $157,500
Over $200,000 but not over $500,000	$45,689.50 plus 35% of the excess over $200,000
Over $500,000	$150,689.50 plus 37% of the excess over $500,000

Head of Household

If taxable income is:	Then income tax equals:
Not over $13,600	10% of the taxable income
Over $13,600 but not over $51,800	$1,360.00 plus 12% of the excess over $13,600
Over $51,800 but not over $82,500	$5,944.00 plus 22% of the excess over $51,800
Over $82,500 but not over $157,500	$12,698.00 plus 24% of the excess over $82,500
Over $157,500 but not over $200,000	$30,698.00 plus 32% of the excess over $157,500
Over $200,000 but not over $500,000	$44,298.00 plus 35% of the excess over $200,000
Over $500,000	$149,298.00 plus 37% of the excess over $500,000

Married Filing Joint Returns and Surviving Spouses

If taxable income is:	Then income tax equals:
Not over $19,050	10% of the taxable income
Over $19,050 but not over $77,400	$1,905.00 plus 12% of the excess over $19,050
Over $77,400 but not over $165,000	$8,907.00 plus 22% of the excess over $77,400
Over $165,000 but not over $315,000	$28,179.00 plus 24% of the excess over $165,000
Over $315,000 but not over $400,000	$64,179.00 plus 32% of the excess over $315,000
Over $400,000 but not over $600,000	$91,379.00 plus 35% of the excess over $400,000
Over $600,000	$161,379.00 plus 37% of the excess over $600,000

Married Filing Separate Returns

If taxable income is:	Then income tax equals:
Not over $9,525	10% of the taxable income
Over $9,525 but not over $38,700	$952.50 plus 12% of the excess over $9,525
Over $38,700 but not over $82,500	$4,453.50 plus 22% of the excess over $38,700
Over $82,500 but not over $157,500	$14,089.50 plus 24% of the excess over $82,500
Over $157,500 but not over $200,000	$32,089.50 plus 32% of the excess over $157,500
Over $200,000 but not over $300,000	$45,689.50 plus 35% of the excess over $200,000
Over $300,000	$80,689.50 plus 37% of the excess over $300,000

Estates and Trusts

If taxable income is:	Then income tax equals:
Not over $2,550	10% of the taxable income
Over $2,550 but not over $9,150	$255.00 plus 24% of the excess over $2,550
Over $9,150 but not over $12,500	$1,839.00 plus 35% of the excess over $9,150
Over $12,500	$3,011.50 plus 37% of the excess over $12,500

§ 1.02 Unearned Income of Children

Under pre-Act law, special tax rules known as the "kiddie tax," apply to the net unearned income of a child if:

1. The child has not reached the age of 19 by the close of the taxable year, or the child is a full-time student under the age of 24, and either of the child's parents is alive at such time;
2. The child's unearned income exceeds $2,100 in 2017; and
3. The child does not file a joint return.

The kiddie tax applies regardless of whether the child may be claimed as a dependent by either or both parents. For children above age 17, the kiddie tax applies only to children whose earned income does not exceed one-half of the amount of their support.

Under the kiddie tax rules under prior law, the net unearned income of a child was taxed at the parents' tax rates if the parents' tax rates were higher than the tax rates of the child. The remainder of a child's taxable income (*i.e.*, earned income, plus unearned income up to $2,100 in 2017, less the child's standard deduction) was taxed at the child's rates, regardless of whether the kiddie tax applied to the child. For these purposes, unearned income is income other than wages, salaries, professional fees, other amounts received as compensation for personal services rendered, and distributions from qualified disability trusts. In general, a child was eligible to use the preferential tax rates that apply to qualified dividends and capital gains.

The kiddie tax was calculated by computing the "allocable parental tax." This involved adding the net unearned income of the child to the parent's income and then applying the parent's tax rate. A child's "net unearned income" was the child's unearned income less the sum of:

1. The minimum standard deduction allowed to dependents; and
2. The greater of such minimum standard deduction amount or the amount of allowable itemized deductions that are directly connected with the production of the unearned incomes.

Beginning on January 1, 2018, the taxable income of a child attributable to earned income is taxed under the rates for single individuals, and taxable income of a child attributable to net unearned income is taxed according to the brackets applicable to trusts and estates (see § 1.01 above). This rule applies to the child's ordinary income and any income taxed at preferential rates. Therefore, under the new law, the child's tax is unaffected by the tax situation of the child's parent or the unearned income of any siblings.

Comment: Note that a child's "kiddie tax" is no longer affected by the tax situation of his or her parent or the unearned income of any siblings. The effect of this change is that the unearned income of children (think interest on a savings or investment account or any kind of income that a child doesn't earn from a job) is taxed at the generally higher rate applicable to trusts and estates.

§ 1.03 Capital Gains

The new law generally retains the prior law maximum rates on net capital gains and qualified dividends. The breakpoints between the zero and 15% rates ("15% breakpoint") and the 15 and 20% rates ("20% breakpoint") are the same amounts as the breakpoints under prior law, except that the breakpoints are indexed using new inflation adjustment factors.

In 2018, the 15% breakpoint is $77,200 for joint returns and surviving spouses (one-half of this amount ($38,600) for married taxpayers filing separately), $51,700 for heads of household, $2,600 for estates and trusts, and $38,600 for other unmarried individuals. The 20% breakpoint is $479,000 for joint returns and surviving spouses (one-half of this amount for married taxpayers filing separately), $452,400 for heads of household, $12,700 for estates and trusts, and $425,800 for other unmarried individuals.

Therefore, in the case of an individual (including an estate or trust) with an adjusted net capital gain, to the extent the gain would not result in taxable income exceeding the 15% breakpoint, such gain is not taxed. Any adjusted net capital gain that would result in taxable income exceeding the 15% breakpoint, but not exceeding the 20% breakpoint, is taxed at 15%. The remaining adjusted net capital gain is taxed at 20%. As under prior law, unrecaptured gain generally is taxed at a maximum rate of 25%, and the 28% rate gain is taxed at a maximum rate of 28%.

Gain from the sale or exchange of a capital asset, such as stock, may receive the preferential tax treatment afforded long-term capital gains if certain conditions are satisfied. Whether or not a sale or exchange has taken place for income tax purposes must be ascertained from all of the relevant facts and circumstances, and the form of an agreement does not necessarily determine whether payments should be treated as ordinary income or capital gains. Instead, the tax consequences depend on the substance of the transaction rather than its form.

If the property is held for more than 12 months prior to the sale, the gain will be classified as long-term capital gain. If the property is held for one year or less, its sale or exchange results in a short-term capital gain or loss. Both net short-term and net long-term capital losses are combined for purposes of offsetting ordinary income.

The Internal Revenue Code does not provide a definition of the term "capital asset" beyond stating that the term refers to "property held by the taxpayer (whether or not connected with a trade or business)." Instead, the term "capital asset" is defined by *what it is not*. Capital assets are property held by a taxpayer (whether or not connected with a trade or business) *other than* property falling into one of the following categories:

- Stock in trade of the taxpayer or other property of a kind which would properly be included in the inventory of the taxpayer if on hand at the close of the tax year;
- Property held by the taxpayer primarily for sale to customers in the ordinary course of the taxpayer's trade or business. The purpose of this exclusion is to differentiate between gain derived from the everyday operations of a business and gain derived from assets that have appreciated in value over a substantial period of time;
- Depreciable property used in a trade or business even if it is fully depreciated;
- Real property used in a taxpayer's trade or business;
- Self-created intangibles such as copyrights, literary, musical or artistic compositions, letters or memorandum or similar property held by the taxpayer who created it, or by one whose basis in the property is determined by reference to the basis of the one who created it, or, in the case of a letter, memorandum or similar property, a taxpayer for whom such property was prepared or produced. A taxpayer may also elect to treat musical compositions and copyrights in musical works as capital assets;
- Accounts or notes receivable acquired in the ordinary course of a trade or business for services rendered or from the sale of stock in trade or property held for sale to customers;
- A U.S. Government publication (including the Congressional Record) held by a taxpayer who received it other than by purchase at a price at which the publication is offered to the public;
- Certain commodities derivative financial instruments held by commodities derivatives dealers unless the instrument has no relationship to the dealer's activities as a dealer and the instrument is shown in the records of the dealer on the date of acquisition as not being held by the dealer as part of the dealer's ordinary business activities;
- Hedging transactions; and
- Supplies of a type regularly consumed by the taxpayer in the ordinary course of a trade or business.

In 2017, the following capital gains rates applied to sales or exchanges by individuals of capital assets that were held for more than 12 months and applied for both regular income tax and alternative minimum tax (AMT) purposes:

- 0% applied to the adjusted net capital gains of individuals if the gain would otherwise be subject to the 10% or 15% ordinary income tax rate;
- 15% applied to adjusted net capital gains of individuals if the gain would otherwise be subject to the 25%, 28%, 33%, or 35% ordinary income tax rate;
- 20% applied to adjusted net capital gains of individuals if the gain would otherwise be subject to the 39.6% ordinary income tax rate. Individuals were subject to the 39.6% percent ordinary income tax rate in 2017 to the extent their taxable income exceeded the applicable threshold amount of $470,700 for married individuals filing joint returns and surviving spouses, $444,550 for heads of households, $418,400 for single individuals, and $235,350 for married individuals filing separate returns.

Additional 3.8% Net Investment Income Tax. Higher-income taxpayers must also pay a 3.8% additional tax on net investment income (NII) to the extent certain threshold amounts of income are exceeded ($200,000 for single filers, $250,000 for joint returns and surviving spouses, $125,000 for married taxpayers filing separately). Therefore, taxpayers within the NII surtax range must pay an additional 3.8% on capital gain, whether long-term or short-term. The effective top rate for net capital gains for many higher-income taxpayers thus became 23.8% (20% + 3.8%) for long-term gain and 43.4% (39.6% + 3.8%) for short-term capital gains in 2017.

Note the following pertaining to certain capital assets:

- a 28% tax rate was imposed on long-term capital gain from the sale or exchange of a collectible even if the collectible was held for more than 12 months. The term "collectibles" is defined as works of art, rugs, antiques, metals, gems, coins, stamps, alcoholic beverages, and any other tangible personal property specified by the IRS. For capital gains purposes, collectibles also include certain coins and bullion.
- a 25% tax gain was imposed on long-term capital gains from the sale or exchange of small business stock gain. Noncorporate taxpayers were able to exclude from gross income 100% of capital gain from the sale or exchange of qualified small business stock (QSBS) that was acquired after September 27, 2010 and held for more than five years. The percentage of excluded capital gain was not used in computing your long-term capital gain or loss, and it was not investment income for purposes of the investment interest limitation. The percentage of capital gain that was not excluded was taxed at the maximum 28% capital gains rate.

- a 25% tax gain was imposed on long-term capital gains attributable to certain prior depreciation that had been claimed on real property.

The new law provides that for the eight-year period beginning on January 1, 2018 and before January 1, 2026, the maximum rates that apply under pre-tax law to net capital gains and qualified dividends will be retained. The new law retains the breakpoints that exist under pre-Act law, but indexes them for inflation beginning in 2018.

Therefore, in 2018, the following capital gains tax rules are applicable:

- The 0% tax rate applies to adjusted net capital gain up to $77,200 for joint filers and surviving spouses, $51,700 for heads of household, $38,600 for single filers, $38,600 for married taxpayers filing separately, and $2,600 for estates and trusts;
- The 15% tax rate applies to adjusted net capital gain over the amount subject to the 0% rate, and up to $479,000 for joint filers and surviving spouses, $452,400 for heads of household, $425,800 for single filers, $239,500 for married taxpayers filing separately, and $12,700 for estates and trusts; and
- The 20% tax rate applies to adjusted net capital gain over $479,000 for joint filers and surviving spouses, $452,400 for heads of household, $425,800 for single filers, $239,500 for married taxpayers filing separately, and $12,700 for estates and trusts.

If an individual taxpayer (including an estate or trust) has an adjusted net capital gain that is less than the breakpoint for application of the 15 and 20% tax rates, the taxpayer's capital gain will not be taxed. Any adjusted net capital gain which would result in taxable income exceeding the 15% breakpoint but not exceeding the 20% breakpoint is taxed at 15%. The remaining adjusted net capital gain is taxed at 20%. As under present law, unrecaptured gain generally is taxed at a maximum tax rate of 25%, and the 28% rate gain is taxed at a maximum rate of 28%.

The additional 3.8% NII tax and the 25 and 28% rate groups are not affected by the new law, and remain unchanged for 2018.

§ 1.04 Exclusions from Definition of Capital Asset

As discussed above, under the old law, certain assets are specifically excluded from the definition of a capital asset, including inventory property, depreciable property, and certain self-created intangibles (*e.g.*, copyrights, musical compositions).

The new law provides that, effective for dispositions beginning on January 1, 2018, the definition of "capital asset" is amended to exclude the following self-created property: patents, inventions, models or designs (whether or not patented), and secret formulas or processes, which are held either by the taxpayer who created the property or by a taxpayer with a substituted or transferred basis from the taxpayer who created the property or for whom the property was created.

> **Caution:** Although patents are excluded from the definition of capital asset under the new law, a qualified holder's gain on the disposition of a patent to an unrelated person may still be taxed at the lowest capital gain tax rate. Qualified holders include the creator of the patent and persons who provided financial backing to the creator.

§ 1.05 Standard Deduction

Under the old law, taxpayers were allowed to reduce their adjusted gross income (AGI) by using either the standard deduction or the sum of their itemized deductions to determine their taxable income. The standard deduction is the sum of the basic standard deduction and, if applicable, the additional standard deduction. The basic standard deduction varied depending on the taxpayer's filing status.

In 2017, the standard deduction amounts were as follows:

Filing Status	Standard Deduction
Married Individuals Filing Joint Returns and Surviving Spouses	$12,700
Heads of Households	$9,350
Unmarried Individuals (other than Surviving Spouses and Heads of Households)	$6,350
Married Individuals Filing Separate Returns	$6,350

Additional Standard Deductions. A taxpayer who, at the end of the tax year, has attained age 65 or is blind, is entitled to an additional standard deduction amount. The additional standard deduction amount is the sum of the additional amount for the aged and the additional amount for the blind. If an individual satisfies the requirements for both the additional amount for the aged and the additional amount for the blind, the taxpayer is entitled to claim both amounts. In 2017, the additional standard deduction amount for the aged or the blind was $1,250. The additional standard deduction amount was increased to $1,550 in 2017 if the individual is also unmarried and not a surviving spouse.

Dependent's Standard Deduction. In 2017, the standard deduction amount for an individual who may be claimed as a dependent by another taxpayer could not exceed the greater of (1) $1,050, or (2) the sum of $350 and the individual's earned income.

Taxpayers Ineligible to Claim Standard Deduction. The following taxpayers may not claim the standard deduction:

1. Married taxpayers filing separately if either spouse itemizes deductions;
2. Nonresident aliens;
3. Individuals who file returns for periods of less than 12 months because of a change in accounting period; and
4. Estates or trusts, common trust funds, or partnerships.

For the eight tax years beginning after December 31, 2017 and before January 1, 2026, the new law provides that the standard deduction is increased as follows:

Filing Status	Standard Deduction
Married Individuals Filing Joint Returns and Surviving Spouses	$24,000
Heads of Households	$18,000
Unmarried Individuals (other than Surviving Spouses and Heads of Households)	$12,000
Married Individuals Filing Separate Returns	$12,000

These standard deduction amounts are adjusted for inflation in tax years beginning after 2018. No changes are made to the current-law additional standard deduction for the elderly and the blind (though they are inflation-adjusted for 2018 to $1,300 for married taxpayers and $1,600 for unmarried taxpayers).

Practical Tip. Taxpayers who find that their mortgage interest, allowable medical expenses, $10,000 of state and local taxes, and charitable contributions do not add up to more than $12,000 (individual) or $24,000 (married filing jointly), should take the standard deduction in 2018.

§ 1.06 Personal and Dependency Exemptions

Under the old law, taxpayers determined their taxable income by subtracting from their adjusted gross income any personal exemption deductions. Personal exemptions generally were allowed for the taxpayer, the taxpayer's spouse, and any dependents. The amount deductible for each personal exemption was scheduled to be $4,150 for 2018 (increased from $4,050 in 2017) and was subject to a phase-out for higher earners. In 2017, the personal exemption was phased out for taxpayers with the following adjusted gross income amounts:

Filing Status	AGI—Beginning of Phase-out	AGI—Completed Phase-out
Married Individuals Filing Joint Returns and Surviving Spouses	$313,800	$436,300
Heads of Households	$287,650	$410,150
Unmarried Individuals (other than Surviving Spouses and Heads of Households)	$261,500	$384,000
Married Individuals Filing Separate Returns	$156,900	$218,150

The amount of tax required to be withheld by employers from a taxpayer's wages was based in part on the number of withholding exemptions a taxpayer claimed on his Form W– 4. An employee was entitled to the following exemptions: (1) an exemption for himself, unless he allowed to be claimed as a dependent of another person; (2) an exemption to which the employee's spouse would be entitled, if that spouse does not file a Form W– 4 for that tax year claiming an exemption described in (1); (3) an exemption for each individual who was a dependent (but only if the employee's spouse had not also claimed such a withholding exemption on a Form W–4); (4) additional withholding allowances (taking into account estimated itemized deductions, estimated tax credits, and additional deductions as provided by the IRS); and (5) a standard deduction allowance.

Under the new law, for tax years beginning after December 31, 2017 and before January 1, 2026, the deduction for personal exemptions is effectively suspended by reducing the exemption amount to zero. A number of corresponding changes are made throughout the Code where specific provisions contain references to the personal exemption amount and, in each of these instances, the dollar amount to be used is $4,150, as adjusted by inflation.

The Conference Agreement released by Congress allows the IRS to administer the withholding rules for tax years beginning before January 1, 2019 without regard to the above amendments—*i.e.*, wage withholding rules may remain the same as present law for 2018. However, the IRS has announced its intention to release updated withholding information early in 2018 to allow people to experience the effects of the new law directly in their paychecks in 2018.

§ 1.07 Return Requirements for Individuals/Filing Thresholds

Under the old law, an unmarried individual is required to file a tax return if the individual had income that equaled or exceeded the personal exemption amount plus the standard deduction applicable to that individual. A married individual entitled to file a joint return was generally required to do so if that individual's gross income, when combined with the individual's spouse's gross income, was less than twice the sum of the exemption amount plus the basic standard deduction applicable to a joint return.

Under the new law, the rules for determining who is required to file a tax return for tax years beginning after December 31, 2017 and before January 1, 2026, are modified. With respect to an individual who is not married (single or head of household), the individual is required to file a tax return if the individual's gross income for the tax year exceeds the applicable standard deduction. Married individuals reach the filing threshold if that individual's gross income, when combined with the individual's spouse's gross income for the tax year, is more than the standard deduction applicable to a joint return, provided that:

1. The individual and his or her spouse, at the close of the tax year, had the same household as their home;
2. The individual's spouse does not file a separate return; and
3. Neither the individual nor his or her spouse is a dependent of another taxpayer who has income (other than earned income) in excess of the amount provided ($1,050 for 2018, as indexed for inflation).

§ 1.08 Repeal of Obamacare Individual Health Care Mandate

Under the Affordable Care Act (also called the ACA or Obamacare) individuals were required to be covered by a health plan that provided at least minimum essential coverage. If they failed to maintain this coverage, they were required to pay a "shared responsibility payment" (also referred to as a penalty) for failure to maintain the coverage (commonly referred to as the "individual mandate" when they filed their federal tax return. Unless an exception applied, the tax was imposed for any month that an individual did not have minimum essential coverage.

Minimum essential coverage included government-sponsored programs (including Medicare, Medicaid, and CHIP, among others), eligible employer-sponsored plans, plans in the individual market, grandfathered group health plans and grandfathered health insurance coverage, and other coverage as recognized by the Secretary of Health and Human Services ("HHS") in coordination with the Secretary of the Treasury. The penalty tax was imposed for any month that an individual did not have minimum essential coverage unless the individual qualified for an exemption.

Comment. Though the tax imposed under the Code is zeroed out, the Code and its regulations will still be relevant because they outline the key concept of minimum essential coverage (MEC). Employers that do not offer their employees MEC under an eligible employer-sponsored plan may still be liable for large employer shared responsibility payments. Individuals who are eligible for MEC for any month do not qualify for the premium tax credit for that month. Reimbursements under qualified small employer health reimbursement arrangements are included in an employee's income unless the employee had MEC.

Under the new law, for months beginning after December 31, 2018, the amount of the individual shared responsibility payment is reduced to zero. This repeal is permanent.

Practical Tip. The IRS has made clear that, in filing your 2017 return, it will not consider your return complete unless you account for your shared responsibility requirement (either because you have health coverage, are exempt from the requirement, or pay the penalty). This will likely apply in 2018 as well.

Comment. Individuals with coverage during the year should receive a reporting form. Marketplace Exchanges are to provide Form 1095-A, *Health Insurance Marketplace Statement*, if the Marketplace provided coverage. An individual with employer or other health coverage ought to receive Form 1095-B, *Health Coverage* (indicating coverage provided), or Form 1095-C, *Employer-Provided Health Insurance Offer and Coverage* (indicating coverage offered or not offered, and coverage provided). These forms can be useful in applying the shared responsibility rules primarily by showing which months (if any) the individual maintained coverage during the year. Presumably, Exchanges will continue to issue Form 1095-A after 2018 since these are necessary for premium tax credit purposes.

§ 1.09 Inflation Adjustment/Changes to Chained Consumer Price Index

Many of the tax amounts and figures that are used in the Internal Revenue Code are annually adjusted to reflect inflation. Under the old law, most of the annual inflation adjustments that were made were based on annual changes in the level of the Consumer Price Index for All Urban Customers (CPI-U). This index measures prices paid by typical urban consumers on a broad range of products and is developed and published by the Department of Labor. Among the inflation-indexed tax parameters are the following individual income tax amounts:

1. The regular income tax brackets;
2. The basic standard deduction;
3. The additional standard deduction for the aged and blind;
4. The personal exemption amount;
5. The thresholds for the overall limitation on itemized deductions and the personal exemption phase-out;
6. The phase-in and phase-out thresholds of the earned income credit;
7. IRA contribution limits and deductible amounts; and
8. The saver's credit.

Under the new law, the dollar amounts that were previously indexed using CPI-U will instead be indexed using the Chained Consumer Price Index for All Urban Consumers. This change is permanent under the new law.

The new Chained Consumer Price Index is a measure of the average change over time in prices paid by urban consumers. It is developed and published by the Department of Labor, but differs from the CPI–U in accounting for the ability of individuals to alter their consumption patterns in response to relative price changes. The Chained Consumer Price Index accomplishes this by allowing for consumer substitution between item categories in the market basket of consumer goods and services that make up the index, while the CPI–U only allows for modest substitution within item categories.

Under the new law, indexed parameters in the Code switch from CPI–U indexing to Chained Consumer Price Index indexing going forward beginning January 1, 2018. Therefore, in the case of any existing tax parameters that are not reset for 2018, the provision indexes parameters as if CPI–U applies through 2017 and Chained Consumer Price Index applies for years thereafter; the provision does not index all existing tax parameters from their base years using the Chained Consumer Price Index. Tax parameters with cost-of-living adjustment base years of 2016 and later are indexed solely with the Chained Consumer Price Index. Therefore, tax values that are reset for 2018 are indexed by the Chained Consumer Price Index beginning January 1, 2019.

Comment. The difference between the two methods of calculating inflation is not insignificant. Between October 2007 and October 2017, the rate of inflation using CPI has been around 18 percent, while the rate of inflation using C-CPI-U has been around 16 percent. Although this difference may appear small, it can have a much larger impact on higher amounts, such as tax bracket income thresholds or the applicable credit amount (unified credit) for estate and gift taxes and the exemption amount for the generation-skipping transfer tax.

§ 1.10   Combat Zone Tax Benefits for Services in Sinai Peninsula of Egypt

Members of the U.S. Armed Forces serving in a combat zone, as designated by Executive Order of the President of the United States, are entitled to numerous tax benefits such as:

1. An exclusion from gross income of certain military pay received for any month during which the member served in a combat zone or was hospitalized as a result of serving in a combat zone;
2. An exemption from taxes on death while serving in a combat zone or dying as a result of wounds, disease, or injury incurred while so serving;
3. Special estate tax rules where death occurs in a combat zone;
4. Special benefits to surviving spouses in the event of a service member's death or missing status;
5. An extension of time limits governing the filing of returns and other rules regarding timely compliance with federal income tax rules; and
6. An exclusion from telephone excise taxes.

Under the new law, the special tax benefits available to members of the Armed Forces serving in a combat zone are expanded so that the Sinai Peninsula of Egypt now qualifies as "qualified hazardous duty area." Therefore, for services provided on or after June 9, 2015 and until January 1, 2026, combat zone tax benefits are granted for the Sinai Peninsula of Egypt, if, as of the enactment date, any member of the U.S. Armed Forces is entitled to special pay (relating to special pay, duty subject to hostile fire or imminent danger), for services performed in such location. This benefit lasts only during the period such entitlement is in effect.

A qualified hazardous duty area is treated in the same manner as if it were a combat zone for purposes of the following provisions of the Code:

1. Exclusions from income for combat zone compensation;
2. Special rule for determining surviving spouse status where the deceased spouse was in missing status as a result of service in a combat zone;

3. Forgiveness of income taxes of members of the military dying in the combat zone or by reason of combat zone incurred wounds;
4. Reduction in estate taxes for members of the military dying in the combat zone or by reason of combat-zone incurred wounds;
5. Exemption from income tax withholding for military pay for any month in which an employee is entitled to the exclusion from income;
6. Exemption from the telephone excise tax for toll telephone service that originates in a combat zone;
7. Special rule permitting filing of a joint return where a spouse is in missing status as a result of service in a combat zone; and
8. Suspension of time provisions.

Comment. Although this combat zone designation impacts a relatively small number of members of the military, this measure providing for combat pay and tax benefits is in light of the heightened volatility in the area and the increased threat from regional groups.

CHAPTER 2

Child Tax Credit

---

§ 2.01 Child Tax Credit

Under the old law, taxpayers who had one or more qualifying children that they could claim as dependents could be entitled to claim a child tax credit in the amount of $1,000 per child. The credit was phased out for higher-income taxpayers and was not adjusted for inflation. The child tax credit is generally a nonrefundable personal credit. All nonrefundable personal tax credits are allowed to the full extent of the taxpayer's regular tax liability, reduced by the foreign tax credit, and alternative minimum tax (AMT) liability.

The child tax credit is generally available to taxpayers with children who are:

1. The taxpayer's qualifying children for purposes of the dependency exemption; and
2. Under age 17 at the close of a calendar year.

For taxpayers with modified adjusted gross income (MAGI) above certain thresholds, the otherwise allowable child tax credit was phased out. The amount of the credit was reduced (but not below zero) by $50 for each $1,000 (or fraction thereof) by which the taxpayer's MAGI exceeded threshold amounts. The threshold amounts, which were not adjusted for inflation, were:

- $110,000 for a joint return;
- $75,000 for an individual who is not married; and
- $55,000 for a married individual filing a separate return.

The term "MAGI" is determined for purposes of the child tax credit without regard to the exclusion from gross income for foreign earned income and foreign housing costs, and the exclusions for income of residents of Guam, American Samoa, the Northern Mariana Islands, and Puerto Rico.

Additional Child Tax Credit. In general, the child tax credit is a non-refundable personal credit which means that it reduces a taxpayer's income tax liability, but any excess will not be refunded to the taxpayer. However, a portion of the child tax credit is treated as a refundable credit. This means that the excess of the child tax credit plus other refundable credits over the taxpayer's tax liability may be refunded to the taxpayer. The amount of the child tax credit that is refundable is called the "additional child tax credit" (ACTC), which is claimed on Schedule 8812.

The credit was refundable in an amount equal to the lesser of the unclaimed portion of the nonrefundable credit amount or 15 percent of the taxpayer's earned income in excess of $3,000 (not adjusted for inflation). The refundable portion of the child tax credit is disallowed for taxpayers electing to exclude any amount of foreign earned income and foreign housing expenses. The calculation of earned income for purposes of determining the additional child tax credit amount takes into account only earned income that is used to determine taxable income.

The calculation of the ACTC depends on whether the taxpayer had at least three qualifying children. For a taxpayer with fewer than three qualifying children, the additional child tax credit was the lesser of:

1. The amount by which the taxpayer's total child tax credit amount exceeded the taxpayer's combined regular and alternative minimum tax liability; or
2. 15 percent of the taxpayer's "earned income" for the tax year that exceeded $3,000.

If the taxpayer had three or more qualifying children, the additional child tax credit is the lesser of:

1. The amount by which the taxpayer's total child tax credit amount exceeded the taxpayer's combined regular and alternative minimum tax liability; or
2. The greater of (i) 15% of the taxpayer's "earned income" for the tax year that exceeded $3,000, or (ii) the excess of the taxpayer's social security taxes for the tax year over the taxpayer's earned income credit. For this purpose, social security taxes are:
    — 50% of self-employment (SECA) tax;
    — The employee's share of FICA tax including amounts treated as such under an agreement entered into by an American employer with respect to foreign affiliates; and
    — The employee's share of railroad retirement tax, including 50% of the tax imposed on employee representatives.

The term "earned income" for purposes of the child tax credit is defined as the sum of wages, salaries, tips, and other taxable employee compensation plus net self-employment earnings. At the taxpayer's election, combat pay may be treated as earned income for this purpose. The definition of "earned income" for purposes of the additional child tax credit is based only on earned income to the extent it is included in computing taxable income.

The sum of the taxpayer's refundable and nonrefundable child tax credit could not exceed $1,000 per qualifying child. For purposes of the overall limit on a taxpayer's nonrefundable credits, the additional child tax credit is not treated as a nonrefundable credit. For instance, if the taxpayer was entitled to a nonrefundable child tax credit of $1,200 and an additional child tax credit of $800, only the $1,200 nonrefundable credit is taken into account in determining the overall limit on nonrefundable credits.

A taxpayer claiming the credit must include a valid Taxpayer Identification Number (TIN) for each qualifying child on the return where the credit is claimed. In most cases, the TIN is the child's Social Security Number (SSN), although Individual Taxpayer Identification Numbers (ITINs) may also be accepted. Taxpayers will be denied the credit if they fail to include the qualifying child's name and tax identification number. The credit will also be denied if the tax identification number was issued after the due date for filing the tax return for that year.

Under the new law, the child tax credit is expanded, effective for tax years beginning after December 31, 2017 and before January 1, 2026. The following changes were made:

- The amount of the child tax credit is increased to $2,000 per qualifying child; The income levels at which the credit phases out are increased to $400,000 for married taxpayers filing jointly ($200,000 for all other taxpayers) (not indexed for inflation). A $500 nonrefundable credit is provided for certain non-child dependents;

- The portion of the child tax credit that is refundable after 2017 and before 2026 is still referred to as the additional child tax credit (ACTC) but is limited to $1,400 per qualifying child, and this amount is indexed for inflation, up to the $2,000 base credit amount. The earned income threshold for the refundable portion of the credit is decreased from $3,000 to $2,500;

- A taxpayer will only be able to claim the child tax credit or the additional child tax credit if the taxpayer includes a Social Security number for each qualifying child for whom the credit is claimed on the tax return. The Social Security number must be issued before the due date for the filing of the tax return where the credit is claimed.

Planning Tip. The time is now. In 2018, taxpayers with children should take advantage of the newly-expanded child tax credit. The new tax law increased the credit amount for each qualifying child to $2,000, increased the phase-out threshold to $400,000 if married filing jointly ($200,000 for other taxpayers), and provided a $500 nonrefundable credit for each dependent who is not a qualifying child. The refundable portion of the credit (additional child tax credit) is limited to $1,400 per qualifying child, but is indexed for inflation and the earned income threshold is reduced to $2,500. Note that parents must include a qualifying child's Social Security number on his or her return to receive the nonrefundable or refundable portion of the credit with respect to the child.

CHAPTER 3

Education and Disability Benefits

§ 3.01 Qualified Tuition Plans (529 Plans)

A qualified tuition program is a popular tax-advantaged college savings program available to investors under Code Sec. 529. These plans are established and maintained by a state instrumentality (such as a brokerage house) under which an individual may make cash contributions to an account established solely to pay the "qualified higher education expenses" of the designated beneficiary of the account. The popularity of college savings plans or "529 plans" (named after the tax code section creating them in 1996) skyrocketed after tax law changes made withdrawals tax-free when the proceeds are used solely to fund the "qualified higher education expenses" of the designated beneficiary of the account.

The 529 plan is available to all taxpayers regardless of how much money they report on their income tax return. Unlike all other education-related tax incentives, no income limit or phase-out applies to 529 plans. The two types of 529 plans available to investors are the college savings plan and the prepaid tuition plan. The more popular college funding option is the 529 college savings plan. With this plan, taxpayers make contributions to an account which is established to meet the *qualified higher education expenses* of a designated beneficiary. Contributions are invested by the selected brokerage house pursuant to any investment option chosen by the account holder and the account balance is available to pay tuition and other qualified educational expenses of the beneficiary when needed. The investment choice may be changed once per calendar year and when the designated beneficiary of the account changes. Funds in the plan can be used to pay for qualified higher education expenses at any eligible college, university, or vocational school in the United States.

Contributions to Qualified Tuition Plan. Contributions made by taxpayers to college savings plans are not deductible for federal income tax purposes, although they may be deductible for state income tax purposes depending on state law. All distributions, including the earnings, are tax-free, provided they are used to pay for qualified higher education expenses. Distributions not used for qualified higher education expenses for reasons other than the death or disability of the designated beneficiary or to the extent that the distribution exceeds amounts not covered by scholarships are subject to tax as well as an additional 10% penalty. Contributions to a qualified tuition program must be made in cash. There is no specific dollar amount imposed on the contributions, account balances, or prepaid tuition benefits relating to a qualified tuition account; however, the program must have adequate safeguards to prevent contributions in excess of amounts necessary to provide for the beneficiary's "qualified higher education expenses."

Prepaid Tuition Plans. Prepaid tuition plans provide incentives for residents to attend in-state colleges and universities. They permit taxpayers to purchase tuition credits or certificates that entitle a designated beneficiary to the waiver of tuition or payment of qualified higher education expenses. With this plan, a parent or grandparent purchases a specific amount of future tuition (*e.g.,* 12 credit hours) at today's prices. A prepaid tuition plan often requires that either the parent or child reside in the state that sponsors the plan and many plans even impose a penalty if the student uses the credits to attend a private or out-of-state college. The advantage of prepaid tuition plans is that they are relatively safe investments. They give families a steady, safe, and modest return on their investment and are typically backed up by the full faith and credit of the state sponsoring the plan. They will only be attractive to parents who want to avoid the risk of market volatility and whose children are near college age and hope to attend an in-state school. Parents seeking a more attractive return on their investment and who don't want to limit college choices to in-state schools, should invest in a college savings plan. A prepaid tuition plan may be established and maintained by one or more "eligible education institutions," including some private colleges and universities. The income exclusion applies for distributions from qualified private plans to the extent the amounts distributed are used for qualified higher education expenses.

Tax Treatment. The 529 plan is an entity that will not be subject to tax provided it does not engage in any unrelated business activities. Earnings on amounts invested in 529 plans grow tax-free. Distributions are generally tax-free to the extent the distributed amounts are used for "qualified higher education expenses." Any excess amount will be subject to tax at the student's income tax rate, which typically will be lower than the parent or grandparent's tax rate thus offering investors an opportunity to shift income to taxpayers in lower tax brackets. Contributions generally are treated as a completed gift eligible for the gift tax annual exclusion. Contributions are not tax deductible for federal income tax purposes, although they may be deductible for state income tax purposes.

"Qualified Higher Education Expenses." Money invested in a 529 plan may be used to pay a student's "qualified higher education expenses," which include tuition, fees, books, supplies, and equipment required for the enrollment or attendance of a designated beneficiary at an eligible educational institution. The cost of computers or peripheral equipment, computer software, and internet access and related services also qualify as "higher education expenses." The computers, equipment, software, or services must be used primarily by the beneficiary while the beneficiary is enrolled at an eligible educational institution.

A student's expenses for room and board will be considered "qualified higher education expenses" if the student is:

1. Enrolled in a degree, certificate, or other program leading to a recognized educational credential at an eligible educational institution; and
2. The student is carrying at least half of the normal full-time workload for the course of study that the student is pursuing. If the student lives at home with his or her parents, room and board costs are the amount determined by the institution. If the student resides in housing owned or operated by the school, room and board costs will be a standard allowance based on the amount that most of the school's residents are normally charged for room and board. For all other students, room and board costs will be the amount of expenses reasonably incurred by the student for room and board.

The amount of room and board treated as qualified higher education expenses cannot exceed the greater of (1) the allowance for room and board included in the eligible educational institution's cost of attendance or (2) the actual invoice amount the student residing in housing owned or operated by the eligible educational institution is charged by the institution for room and board.

"Eligible Educational Institution." Money invested in a 529 plan can be used to cover qualified expenses at an eligible educational institution which is generally an accredited postsecondary educational institution offering credit toward a bachelor's degree, an associate's degree, a graduate-level or professional degree, or other recognized postsecondary credential. Certain proprietary institutions and postsecondary vocational institutions are also eligible institutions provided the institution is eligible to participate in Department of Education student aid programs.

Rollovers. Amounts in one 529 plan may be transferred tax-free from one plan for the benefit of a designated beneficiary to another qualified tuition program for the same beneficiary. This rollover will not be considered a distribution. However, the tax-free rollover treatment only applies to one transfer within any 12-month period with respect to the same beneficiary. Amounts in a college savings plan may be rolled over tax-free to an account for another beneficiary who must be: (1) of the same (or higher) generation as the original beneficiary; and (2) a member of the same family. The tax code provides a lengthy list of family members who qualify, including the original beneficiary's spouse, parents, children, stepchildren, grandchildren, siblings, first cousins, nieces and nephews, aunts and uncles, and all in-laws.

The new law allows such plans to distribute up to $10,000 in expenses for tuition incurred during the year in connection with the enrollment or attendance of the designated beneficiary at a public, private or religious elementary or secondary school. This limitation applies on a per-student basis, rather than a per-account basis. Thus, under this provision, although an individual may be the designated beneficiary of multiple accounts, that individual may receive a maximum of $10,000 in distributions free of tax, regardless of whether the funds are distributed from a single or multiple accounts. Any excess distributions received by the individual would be treated as a distribution subject to tax. This change applies to distributions made after December 31, 2017.

> **Planning Tip.** If you have a 529 plan for your child who attends a public, private or religious elementary or secondary school, you should now use funds from the 529 plan to pay tuition for the elementary or secondary school student. The new law modifies 529 qualified tuition plans to allow the plans to distribute no more than $10,000 in tuition expenses incurred during the tax year for designated beneficiaries enrolled at a public, private or religious elementary or secondary school. The limit on how much can be distributed from the 529 plan free of tax is $10,000, even if the funds are distributed from multiple 529 accounts.

§ 3.02 Discharge of Debt Income for Student Loans

Income from discharge of indebtedness (also called cancellation of debt) is included in the general definition of gross income. The concept of discharge of indebtedness income is that a taxpayer has realized an accession to income—to the extent that he has been released from indebtedness—because assets previously offset by the liability arising from the indebtedness have been freed. Essentially, the taxpayer has earned money by not having to pay money. Therefore, based on these principles, taxpayers who have a commercial, private lender or employer discharge part or all of their debt must include the amount that was discharged in income as cancellation of debt (COD) income unless an exception or exclusion applies.

Students whose loans are forgiven (in whole or in part) because they worked in a designated profession for any of a broad class of employers generally need not include the discharged debt in income.

For purposes of the exclusion, a student loan is any loan to an individual designed to assist the student in attending an educational organization that qualifies for a tax exemption. Specifically, the loan must be made by one of the following lenders:

1. The United States or one of its instrumentalities or agencies;
2. A state, territory, or possession of the United States, or the District of Columbia, or any "political subdivision of the state;"
3. A state, county, or municipal hospital that is controlled by a tax-exempt public benefit corporation and whose employees are deemed public employees under state law;
4. Any tax-exempt educational organization that originally received the funds from which the loans were made from the United States, a state, or a tax-exempt public benefit corporation; or
5. An exempt educational organization that is designed to encourage its students to serve in occupations with unmet needs or in areas with unmet needs and under which the services provided by the students or former students are for or under the direction of a governmental unit or a tax-exempt organization.

The exclusion applies to forgiveness of loans made by educational organizations and tax-exempt organizations to refinance any existing student loans, and not just loans made by educational organizations, but only if made under a program of the refinancing organization that requires the student to fulfil a public service requirement under the direction of a governmental entity or tax-exempt organization.

Student loans eligible for this special income-exclusion rule must be made to an individual to assist the individual in attending an educational institution that normally maintains a regular faculty and curriculum and normally has a regularly enrolled body of students in attendance at the place where its education activities are regularly carried on. Loan proceeds may be used not only for tuition and required fees, but also to cover room and board expenses.

In addition, an individual's gross income does not include amounts from the forgiveness of loans made by educational organizations (and certain tax-exempt organizations in the case of refinancing loans) out of private, nongovernmental funds if the proceeds of such loans are used to pay costs of attendance at an educational institution or to refinance any outstanding student loans (not just loans made by educational organizations) and the student is not employed by the lender organization. In the case of such loans made or refinanced by educational organizations (or refinancing loans made by certain tax-exempt organizations), cancellation of the student loan must be contingent on the student working in an occupation or area with unmet needs and such work must be performed for, or under the direction of, a tax-exempt charitable organization or a governmental entity.

The new law provides that effective January 1, 2018 and before January 1, 2026, student loan discharges will be excluded from gross income even if the student loans were discharged because of the student's death or total and permanent disability.

§ 3.03 Contributions and Rollovers to ABLE Accounts

In the Achieve a Better Living Experience Act of 2014 (ABLE), Congress provided a tax-advantaged savings program specifically targeted to persons with disabilities. Beginning on January 1, 2015, states were able to establish tax-exempt ABLE accounts to assist persons with disabilities in paying qualified disability-related expenses on behalf of designated beneficiaries with disabilities. The ABLE account is designed to supplement, but not supplant, benefits provided through private insurance, Medicaid, SSI, the beneficiary's employment, and other sources. The disabled individual is the designated beneficiary and owner of that account.

Generally, contributions to the ABLE account are subject to both an annual and a cumulative limit and when made by a person other than the designated beneficiary are treated as nontaxable gifts to the designated beneficiary. Distributions made from an ABLE account for qualified disability expenses of the designated beneficiary are not included in the designated beneficiary's gross income. The earnings portion of distributions from the ABLE account in excess of the qualified disability expenses is includible in the gross income of the designated beneficiary. An ABLE account may be used for the long-term benefit and/or short-term needs of the designated beneficiary.

A qualified ABLE program is one established and maintained by a state, agency or instrumentality of the state that allows a person to make contributions to an ABLE account to pay the qualified disability expenses of the account's designated beneficiary.

The requirement that a state can only establish an ABLE account for a designated beneficiary residing in the state or a contracting state was eliminated in 2015. Thus, nonresidents of the state that established and maintain the ABLE program can be designated beneficiaries of a state's ABLE accounts.

Since the residency requirement has been eliminated, ABLE programs no longer need to include the state of residency of the designated beneficiary in the notice of the establishment of the ABLE account provided to the IRS.

In addition, the ABLE program must satisfy the following requirements:

1. All contributions must be in cash and the aggregate of all annual contributions cannot exceed the annual gift tax exclusion amount (estimated to be $15,000 in 2018);
2. Provide for separate accounting for each designated beneficiary;
3. Provide that any contributor or designated beneficiary may directly or indirectly control the investment of any contribution or earnings no more than twice a year;
4. Provide that no interest in, or portion of, an ABLE account can be pledged as security for a loan; and
5. Have in place safeguards to prevent aggregate total contributions, including contributions from any prior ABLE program on behalf of a designated beneficiary from exceeding state limits for its qualified tuition program with respect to the amount necessary to provide for a beneficiary's qualified higher education expenses.

A qualified ABLE program is allowed to provide services to residents of other states that do not have a qualified ABLE program and have entered into a contract with a state with a qualified ABLE program to provide access to their residents.

"Eligible Individuals" Defined. An individual will be eligible to create an ABLE account if he or she is disabled or blind, and the onset of the disability or blindness occurred before the individual reached age

26. The person must either be entitled to benefits based on blindness or disability under title II of the Social Security Act or the person must have a disability certificate on file with the IRS for the year. The disability certificate need not be provided to the IRS when opening an ABLE account but the beneficiary must provide a signed statement under penalty of perjury stating that he or she is eligible and stating further that he or she has a diagnosis statement signed by a physician in his or her records. The certificate must state that the beneficiary is blind or has a medically determinable physical or mental impairment resulting in "marked and severe functional limitations" that can be expected to result in death, or that has lasted or can be expected to last for a continuous period of not less than 12 months.

Tax Treatment. Contributions to an ABLE account are not deductible and are limited to the amount of the annual gift tax exclusion. Distributions are excludable from gross income if used to pay qualifying disability expenses. A qualified ABLE program is exempt from taxation, except for taxes imposed on any unrelated business taxable income (UBTI). Money in an ABLE account is disregarded for purposes of federal-means testing for claiming benefits under other federal welfare benefit programs with certain exceptions.

Tax Treatment on Distributions. Distributions from an ABLE account for a tax year are not includible in gross income unless they exceed the amount of qualified disability expenses incurred during the tax year. If the distribution is in excess of qualified disability expenses, the amount includible in gross income is the excess amount reduced by an amount in the same ratio as the expenses bear to the distributions. Distributions from an ABLE account that are used for nonqualified expenses are subject to income tax on the portion of such distributions attributable to earnings from the account, plus a 10% penalty on that portion. This 10% addition to tax does not apply if the payment or distribution is made to the designated beneficiary, or to the estate of the designated beneficiary on or after the death of the designated beneficiary.

"Qualified Disability Expenses" Defined. "Qualified disability expenses" are defined as expenses incurred that relate to the blindness or disability of the designated beneficiary of the ABLE account and are for the benefit of that designated beneficiary in maintaining or improving his or her health, independence, or quality of life. Such expenses include, but are not limited to, expenses related to the designated beneficiary's education, housing, transportation, employment training and support, assistive technology and related services, personal support services, health, prevention and wellness, financial management and administrative services, legal fees, expenses for oversight and monitoring, and funeral and burial expenses.

Qualified disability expenses include basic living expenses and are not limited to items for which there is a medical necessity or which solely benefit a disabled individual. For example, if an individual, has a medically determined mental impairment that causes marked and severe limitations on her ability to navigate and communicate and a smart phone would enable her to perform those functions more safely and effectively, thereby helping her to maintain her independence and to improve her quality of life, the expense of buying, using, and maintaining a smart phone that is used by her would be considered a qualified disability expense.

Rollovers. Amounts in ABLE accounts can generally be rolled tax-free only into another ABLE account for the same individual or into an ABLE account for a family member who is also an eligible individual who is blind or disabled and became so before turning 26, and is entitled to benefits under the SSI or SSDI programs. To escape tax, the amount distributed must be rolled over into another ABLE account no later than the 60th day after the date of payment or distribution. The ABLE account accepting the payment must be established for the designated beneficiary or an eligible family member. In the event of a change of designated beneficiary, taxation of the payment or distributions will be avoided if the new beneficiary is an eligible individual for the tax year and a member of the family of the former designated beneficiary. Tax-fee rollovers for purposes of changing programs or changing the designated beneficiary are limited to one such transfer within a 12-month period which commences on the date of the last transfer of an ABLE account from any qualified ABLE program for the benefit of the designated beneficiary.

§ 3.04 Savers Credit

To encourage taxpayers to establish or maintain private savings accounts to insure adequate savings for retirement, the nonrefundable qualified retirement savings contribution credit (commonly referred to as the saver's credit) may be claimed by eligible taxpayers for contributions or deferrals to retirement savings plans. To be eligible for the saver's credit, a taxpayer who makes a contribution to a qualified retirement savings plan must be at least 18 at the close of the tax year, must *not* be claimed as a dependent on another's tax return, and must *not* be a full-time student. Students who are enrolled for 12 hours or more in any five months of the years are considered to be full-time students and are not eligible for the credit. The amount of the credit is equal to the "applicable percentage" times the amount of qualified retirement savings contributions (not to exceed $2,000) made by an eligible individual in the tax year to certain specified retirement plans.

In 2017, the maximum credit rate was 50%, which was completely phased out when AGI exceeded $62,000 for joint return filers, $46,500 for head of household filers, and $31,000 for single and married filing separately filers.

The "applicable percentage" is the percentage determined in accordance with the following table:

Adjusted Gross Income

Joint return		Head of a household		All other cases		Applicable percentage
Over	Not over	Over	Not over	Over	Not over	
$0	$37,000	$0	$27,750	$0	$18,500	50
37,000	40,000	27,750	30,000	18,500	20,000	20
40,000	62,000	30,000	46,500	20,000	31,000	10
62,000	—	46,500	—	31,000	—	0

The credit may be claimed in addition to any deduction or exclusion that otherwise applies to the contribution. However, the amount of any eligible contribution is reduced by any distributions from a qualified retirement plan or IRA in the year for which the credit is claimed or the two tax years preceding the year in which the credit is claimed. The amount of an otherwise eligible contribution is also reduced by distributions received after the close of the tax year in which the credit is claimed and before the due date for the return for the year of the credit.

§ 3.05 What is the Effect of the Tax Cuts and Jobs Act on These Programs?

Contribution Amount to ABLE Accounts Increased and Rollovers from Qualified Tuition Plans Allowed. The new law provides that effective for tax years beginning after December 22, 2017 and for contributions before January 1, 2026, amounts from 529 plans may be rolled over to an ABLE account without penalty, provided that the ABLE account is owned by the designated beneficiary of the 529 account, or a member of the designated beneficiary's family.   For these purposes, a member of the family means, with respect to any designated beneficiary, the taxpayer's: (1) spouse; (2) child or descendant of a child; (3) brother, sister, stepbrother or stepsister; (4) father, mother or ancestor of either; (5) stepfather or stepmother; (6) niece or nephew; (7) aunt or uncle; (8) in-law; (9) the spouse of any individual described in (2) – (8); and (10) any first cousin of the designated beneficiary.

These rolled-over amounts count towards the overall limitation on amounts that can be contributed to an ABLE account within a taxable year. Any amount rolled over that is in excess of this limitation will be includible in the gross income of the distributee.

After the overall limitation on contributions is reached (*i.e.,* the annual gift tax exemption amount which, for 2018, is $15,000), an ABLE account's designated beneficiary can contribute an additional amount, up to the lesser of (a) the federal poverty line for a one-person household; or (b) the individual's compensation for the tax year.

Saver's Credit Eligible. In addition, the designated beneficiary of an ABLE account can claim the saver's credit for contributions made to his or her ABLE account.

Recordkeeping Requirements. The new law also requires that a designated beneficiary (or person acting on the beneficiary's behalf) maintain adequate records for ensuring compliance with the above limitations.

CHAPTER 4

Personal and Nonbusiness Deductions

§ 4.01 Phase-out of Itemized Deductions

Individual taxpayers are generally given the option to either claim a standard deduction or itemize deductions. Under the old law, the total amount of most otherwise allowable itemized deductions (see exceptions listed below) was limited for certain higher-income taxpayers. For taxpayers who exceed the threshold, the otherwise allowable amount of itemized deductions was reduced by 3% of the amount of the taxpayers' adjusted gross income (AGI) exceeding the threshold. The total reduction couldn't be greater than 80% of all itemized deductions, and certain itemized deductions were exempt from this Pease limitation.

In 2017, the total amount of itemized deductions allowed was reduced by $0.03 for each dollar of AGI in excess of the following phase-out amounts:

- $313,800 for married taxpayers filing a joint return and surviving spouses;
- $287,650 for heads of households;
- $261,500 for single taxpayers who are not surviving spouses or heads of households; and
- $156,900 for married taxpayers filing separate returns.

For purposes of the phase-out, the following deductions are not included in the taxpayer's total itemized deductions and, therefore, are not affected by any phase-out of the taxpayer's allowable itemized deductions:

1. Investment interest expenses;
2. Casualty and theft losses;
3. Allowable wagering losses; and
4. Medical expenses.

All other limitations on itemized deductions, such as the 2-percent floor for miscellaneous itemized deductions, are applied first, and then the otherwise allowable total amount of itemized deductions is reduced. The phase-out is limited to individual taxpayers; it does not apply to estates and trusts.

For tax years beginning after December 31, 2017 and before January 1, 2026, the overall limitation on itemized deductions is suspended. This is good news for higher-income taxpayers, as they have not been able to claim itemized deductions in recent years. Indeed, given that the standard deduction is nearly doubled for 2018 through 2025, it is likely that *only* higher-income taxpayers will be able to take advantage of itemized deductions.

§ 4.02 Mortgage Interest Deduction

Even though personal interest is typically not deductible, an exception is made for interest paid on a home mortgage, which may be claimed by an individual as an itemized deduction. This type of interest is called "qualified residence interest" for tax purposes and this term is defined as interest that is paid or accrued during the tax year on either acquisition indebtedness or home equity indebtedness secured by the taxpayer's qualified residence by a mortgage, deed of trust, or land contract. A qualified residence for this purpose includes the taxpayer's principal residence and one other residence such as a vacation home that is not rented out at any time during the tax year or that is used by the taxpayer for a minimum number of days. A qualified residence can be a house, condominium, cooperative, mobile home, house trailer, or boat.

Acquisition indebtedness is debt incurred in acquiring, constructing or substantially improving a qualified residence of the taxpayer and which secures the residence. Refinanced debt remains acquisition indebtedness to the extent that it does not exceed the principal amount of acquisition indebtedness immediately before refinancing. Under the old law, the total amount that taxpayers could deduct as acquisition indebtedness could not exceed $1 million for any period or $500,000 in the case of a married individual filing separately. No deduction is available for mortgage interest that is capitalized into the principal of a mortgage note and not actually paid by the taxpayer. Included in deductible acquisition indebtedness is interest paid on a builder's construction loan and interest paid on debt to purchase raw land.

"Home equity indebtedness" is any debt other than acquisition indebtedness that is secured by a taxpayer's qualified residence. Interest on such debt was deductible even if the proceeds were used for personal expenditures. Taxpayers could only deduct up to $100,000 of home equity indebtedness, or $50,000 in the case of a married individual filing a separate return. The amount of home equity indebtedness could not exceed the fair market value of the residence reduced by the acquisition indebtedness. Any interest over and above the home equity debt limit would be treated as personal interest and would not be deductible.

Acquisition indebtedness may constitute home equity indebtedness to the extent the debt exceeds the dollar limits for acquisition indebtedness, but subject to the dollar and fair market value limits for home equity indebtedness. Thus, under the old law, an individual could deduct interest paid on up to $1.1 million of such debt ($550,000 if married filing separately) as qualified residence interest. Interest attributable to debt over these limits was nondeductible personal interest.

§ 4.03 Effect of the Tax Cuts and Jobs Act on Home Equity Interest; Acquisition Indebtedness

Under the new law, for tax years beginning after December 31, 2017 and before January 1, 2026, the deduction for interest on home equity indebtedness is suspended, and the deduction for mortgage interest is limited to underlying indebtedness of up to $750,000 ($375,000 for married taxpayers filing separately).

For tax years after December 31, 2025, the prior $1 million/$500,000 limitations are restored, and a taxpayer may treat up to these amounts as deductible acquisition indebtedness regardless of when the indebtedness was incurred. The suspension for deductibility of home equity indebtedness also ends for tax years beginning after December 31, 2025.

In the case of acquisition indebtedness incurred before December 15, 2017, the limitation is $1 million ($500,000 in the case of married taxpayers filing separately). A taxpayer who has entered into a binding written contract before December 15, 2017 to close on the purchase of a principal residence before January 1, 2018, and who purchases such residence before

April 1, 2018, will be considered to have incurred the acquisition indebtedness prior to December 15, 2017.

The $1 million/$500,000 limitations continue to apply to taxpayers who refinance existing qualified residence indebtedness that was incurred before December 31, 2017, so long as the indebtedness resulting from the refinancing doesn't exceed the amount of the refinanced indebtedness.

> **Practical Tip.** If you enter into a binding, written contract to purchase a principal residence before December 15, 2017 to close on the purchase of such residence before January 1, 2018, be sure to actually complete the transaction before April 1, 2018 for it to be considered qualified indebtedness incurred prior to December 15, 2017.

§ 4.04 State and Local Tax Deduction

Under pre-Act law, individual taxpayers could claim a deduction for the following taxes paid or accrued, whether or not they were incurred in a taxpayer's trade or business:

1. State and local real and foreign property taxes;
2. State and local personal property taxes;
3. State, local and foreign income, war, profits, and excess profits taxes.

The individual taxpayer also had the option to make an election to claim an itemized deduction for state and local general sales taxes in lieu of the itemized deduction for state and local income taxes.

The new law provides that for tax years beginning after December 31, 2017 and before January 1, 2026, state, local, and foreign property taxes, and state and local sales taxes, are fully deductible only when paid or accrued in carrying on a trade or business or an activity relating to expenses for the production of income. Therefore, taxpayers may only fully claim deductions for state, local and foreign property taxes, and sales taxes that are presently deductible in computing income on an individual's Schedule C, Schedule E, or Schedule F on the individual's tax return. For example, an individual taxpayer may only deduct property taxes if these taxes were imposed on residential rental property which qualifies as a business asset.

However, a taxpayer may claim an itemized deduction of up to $10,000 ($5,000 for a married taxpayer filing a separate return) for the aggregate of (i) state and local property taxes not paid or accrued in carrying on a trade or business activity; and (ii) state and local income, war profits, and excess profits taxes (or sales taxes in lieu of income, etc. taxes) paid or accrued in the tax year.

Foreign real property taxes may not be deducted under this exception. Congress has preempted a taxpayer's attempt to prepay income tax for a future tax year in order to avoid the dollar limitation applicable for tax years beginning after 2017.

§ 4.05 Deduction for Personal Casualty Losses

Under prior law, indivdual taxpayers could generally claim an itemized deduction for uncompensated personal casualty losses, including those arising from fire, storm, shipwreck, or other casualty, or from theft even though the loss did not occur in a trade or business or in a transaction entered into for profit.

A loss is treated as sustained during the tax year in which the loss occurs, as evidenced by closed and completed transactions and as fixed by identifiable events occurring during that tax year.   A "casualty" is defined as the damage, destruction, or loss of property resulting from an identifiable event that is sudden, unexpected, or unusual. Suddenness is an essential element of a casualty. To be sudden, the event must be one that is swift, not gradual or progressive. An unexpected event is one that is ordinarily unanticipated, unintended and unusual. Taxpayers cannot claim a casualty loss if they lose an article as a result of their own negligence or carelessness.

The amount of a taxpayer's personal casualty loss deduction is the lesser of: (1) the sustained loss which is defined as the property's value just before the casualty less its value immediately afterward, or (2) the adjusted basis of the property for figuring loss on a sale. This amount eligible for a deduction is reduced by:

1. Insurance;
2. Amounts received from an employer or disaster relief agencies to restore the property;
3. Other compensation for lost property;
4. $100 per casualty or theft; if the taxpayer sustains more than one loss from a single event, only one $100 reduction is made. If spouses file jointly, they are treated as one taxpayer. Separate losses sustained by the same act, therefore, bring only one reduction.

In addition, aggregate net casualty and theft losses are deductible only to the extent that they exceed 10% of an individual taxpayer's adjusted gross income.

The new law provides that effective January 1, 2018 and before December 31, 2025, a taxpayer may only claim a personal casualty and theft loss if the loss was attributable to a federally-declared disaster. The government provides a list of areas that are designated as "federally-declared disaster areas" during the year. Amendments expanding the area declared a disaster area are frequently issued. The most recent federally-declared disaster areas can be found at the Federal Emergency Management Agency (FEMA) website at www.fema.gov.

§ 4.06 Limitation on Gambling Loss Deductions

It is well established that gambling winnings, whether legal or illegal, are included in the recipient's gross income. The taxable gains are the amount by which winnings exceed the amount wagered. When the taxpayer cannot establish the amount wagered, the full value of the winnings is included in income. In general, taxpayers can claim a deduction for wagering losses to the extent of wagering winnings.

The tax laws have historically treated gambling losses in one of two ways. Taxpayers engaged in the trade or business of gambling were characterized as professional gamblers and could deduct their gambling losses against their gambling winnings "above the line" as a trade or business expense in arriving at adjusted gross income. In the case of recreational gamblers who were not engaged in the trade or business of gambling, gambling losses were allowable as an itemized deduction, but only to the extent of gambling winnings. If these recreational gamblers claimed the standard deduction instead of itemizing their deductions, they may not have been able to deduct any gambling losses.

In cases where gamblers could show that they engaged in gambling activities with continuity and regularity, conducted their gambling activities in a business-like manner, viewed the activity as work rather than a hobby, and consulted with experts, the Tax Court has held that the taxpayers were professional gamblers and therefore entitled to report gambling winnings and losses on Schedule C, *Profit or Loss from Business* and deduct both wagering costs and gambling-related nonwagering business expenses from gambling winnings.

Nonprofessional gamblers were considered to be merely recreational or casual gamblers, not engaged in the trade or business of gambling and their gambling losses were only deductible as a miscellaneous itemized deduction to the extent of their gambling winnings. If these recreational gamblers claimed the standard deduction instead of itemizing their deductions, they may not have been able to deduct any gambling losses. In determining whether taxpayers are professional or recreational gamblers, the Tax Court has developed a facts and circumstances test. The court will look at the following factors to determine whether the taxpayer is a professional or recreational gambler:

1. Whether the taxpayer engaged in his gambling activities in a business-like manner:
2. Whether the taxpayer attempted to increase his profitability in the activity;
3. Whether the taxpayer maintained records of his gambling transactions;
4. Whether the taxpayer consulted with gambling experts to adjust gambling strategies;
5. Whether the taxpayer showed a profit motive;
6. Whether the taxpayer maintained receipts, books, or records of his gambling activity;
7. Whether the taxpayer maintained daily contemporaneous records of his gambling activities; and
8. Whether the taxpayer's livelihood depended on his gambling activity.

The Tax Cuts and Jobs Act provides that for tax years beginning after December 31, 2017 and before January 1, 2026, the limitation on wagering losses is modified to provide that *all* deductions for expenses incurred in carrying out wagering transactions, not just gambling losses, are limited to the extent of gambling winnings. The provision thus reverses the result reached by the Tax Court where the court held that a taxpayer's expenses incurred in the conduct of the trade or business of gambling, other than the cost of wagers, were not limited to the extent of gambling winnings, and were thus deductible as ordinary and necessary business expenses in the case of the "professional gambler."

§ 4.07 Itemized Deduction of Charitable Contributions by Individuals

Taxpayers may claim an itemized deduction for certain charitable contributions made during the tax year to charities, governments and other qualified organizations. The deduction for an individual's charitable contribution is limited to prescribed percentages of the taxpayer's "contribution base" which is the individual's adjusted gross income computed without regard to any net operating loss carryback. Donors can carry forward for five years their charitable contributions that exceed the deductible limit for the year of the donation. Under the old law, an individual's deductible donations are limited to:

1. 50% of the contribution base, for donations of cash or nonappreciated (ordinary income) property to public charities, private foundations other than nonoperating private foundations, and certain governmental units and other organizations (collectively, "50% organizations");

2. the lesser of (i) 30% of the contribution base or (ii) the excess of 50% of the contribution base over the amount of contributions subject to the 50% limit, for donations of cash or nonappreciated property to nonoperating private foundations or "for the use of" 50% organizations;

3. 30% percent of the contribution base (after taking into account donations other than capital gain property donations), for donations of appreciated capital gain property to 50% organizations; an individual may elect to bring all appreciated capital gain property donations for a tax year within the 50% limit;

4. the lesser of (i) 20% of the contribution base or (ii) the excess of 30% of the contribution base over the amount of contributions subject to the 30% limit, for donations of appreciated capital gain property to nonoperating private foundations; and

5. 20% percent of the contribution base, for donations of capital gain property "for the use of" 50% organizations and nonoperating private foundations.

College Stadium Seats in Exchange for Charitable Donations. Under prior law, a donor who made a charitable donation to or for a college or university and received in return the right to purchase tickets to athletic events in the institution's athletic stadium could deduct 80% of the payment as a charitable contribution. This special treatment did not apply if the donor received tickets instead of the *right to purchase* tickets. Any part of the payment that was for the actual cost of tickets was not deductible.

Substantiation for Donations of $250 or More. Under prior law, no charitable deduction was allowed for contributions of $250 or more unless the donor substantiated the contribution by a contemporaneous written acknowledgment obtained from the donee organization indicating whether the charity provided any good or service to the taxpayer in consideration for the contribution. A donor was not required to obtain the acknowledgment if the donee filed a return with the IRS reporting the information required to be included in a valid acknowledgment. Until final regulations are issued, however, donors must obtain the required substantiation from the donee.

New Law Increases Percentage Limit for Charitable Contributions. The new law provides that for charitable contributions made after December 31, 2017 and before January 1, 2026, the 50% limitation for cash contributions to public charities and certain private foundations is increased to 60%. Contributions exceeding the 60% limitation are generally allowed to be carried forward and deducted for up to five years, subject to the later year's ceiling.

New Law Says No Deduction for Amounts Paid for College Athletic Seating Rights. The new law provides that for contributions made in tax years beginning after December 31, 2017, no charitable deduction would be allowed for any payment to an institution of higher education in exchange for which the payor receives the right to purchase tickets or seating at an athletic event.

New Law Repeals Substantiation Exception. The new law repeals the donee-reporting exemption from the contemporaneous written acknowledgment requirement for tax years beginning after December 31, 2017.

> **Practical Tip:** Consider increasing your charitable contributions. Beginning after December 31, 2017 and before January 1, 2026, the 50 percent limitation for cash contributions to public charities and certain private foundations is increased to 60 percent. Contributions exceeding 60 percent can generally be carried forward and deducted for up to five years, subject to the later year's ceiling. However, remember that the increased standard deduction may mean that, even with an increase in your charitable contribution, it may not be more advantageous to itemize deductions and claim a charitable deduction.

§ 4.08 Itemized Deduction of Medical Expenses

Individual taxpayers could claim an itemized deduction for unreimbursed medical expenses, but only to the extent that such expenses exceeded 10% of the taxpayer's adjusted gross income. For tax years beginning after December 31, 2012, and ending before January 1, 2017, a 7.5-percent-of-AGI floor for medical expenses applied if a taxpayer or the taxpayer's spouse had reached age 65 before the close of the tax year. In the case of married taxpayers, the 7.5 percent threshold applied if either spouse had obtained the age of 65 before the close of the taxable year.

To be deductible, the expenses paid during the tax year must be for the medical care of the taxpayer, the taxpayer's spouse, or one of the taxpayer's dependents. It does not matter when the injury occurred, so long as the taxpayer actually paid (including credit card charges) the medical expenses during the tax year. In addition, the expenses to be deducted by the taxpayer may not be reimbursed by insurance or otherwise. If the medical expenses are reimbursed, then they must be reduced by the reimbursement before the threshold is applied. The amount of premiums paid by the taxpayer for medical insurance may be deducted as a medical expense.

The Code defines expenses for medical care as amounts paid for the diagnosis, cure, mitigation, treatment, or prevention of disease, or for the purpose of affecting any structure or function of the body. The deduction for medical care expenses is confined strictly to expenses incurred primarily for the prevention or alleviation of a physical or mental defect or illness. An expense that is merely beneficial to the general health of an individual is not considered an expense for medical care.

Medical expenses include more than just doctor bills. Medical expenses include a wide variety of costs associated with diagnosing, curing, mitigating, treating, or preventing disease. The medical expense deduction is also available for the cost of related transportation and health insurance.

For purposes of the alternative minimum tax (AMT), medical expenses were only deductible to the extent they exceeded 10% of AGI.

Medical Expense Deduction-AGI Threshold Reduced. For tax years beginning after December 31, 2016 and before January 1, 2019, the new tax law provides that the threshold on medical expense deductions is reduced to 7.5 percent for all taxpayers regardless of age. The 7.5-percent threshold does not apply for purposes of the Alternative Minimum Tax (AMT) (see §8.01) for tax years beginning after December 31, 2016 and before January 1, 2019. Therefore, the threshold for AMT purposes beginning after December 31, 2016 and before January 1, 2019 will be 10%.

> **Practical Tip.** The new law temporarily increases itemized deductions for medical expenses. For 2018 these expenses can be claimed as itemized deductions to the extent they exceed a floor equal to 7.5% of a taxpayer's adjusted gross income (AGI). In 2018, many individuals will have to claim the standard deduction because many itemized deductions will be eliminated, and the standard deduction will be increased. If the taxpayer is planning to itemize deductions and has any elective medical expenses or procedures, he or she should think about acting on those now. For tax years after December 31, 2016 and before January 1, 2019, medical expenses are deductible if in excess of 7.5% of adjusted gross income. After that time, these expenses will only be deductible if in excess of 10% of adjusted gross income.

§ 4.09 Deduction for Alimony

Payments incident to divorce generally fall into one of two categories: alimony or property settlements. In general, alimony is a division of income, and property settlements are a division of marital property. A property settlement is not a taxable event and does not give rise to any gain or loss. In contrast, alimony and separate maintenance payments are deductible above-the-line by the payor-spouse and includible in income by the recipient-spouse. As an above-the-line deduction, alimony has been subtracted directly from the payor's gross income without being limited by the payor's AGI.

The taxpayer who is paying alimony to an ex-spouse (called the payor) has been able to claim a deduction for "alimony or separate maintenance payments." Payments qualified as "alimony or separate maintenance payments" if they were in cash (including a check or money order) and all four of the following requirements were satisfied:

1. The payment was received by (or on behalf of) a spouse under a "divorce or separation instrument;" any payments made in the absence of a divorce or separation instrument were not treated as deductible alimony;
2. The divorce or separation instrument did not designate the payment as one which is not includible in gross income and not allowable as a deduction;
3. In the case of an individual legally separated from his spouse under a decree of divorce or of separate maintenance, the payee-spouse and the payor-spouse are not members of the same household at the time payment is made. However, ex-spouses will not be considered to be living together if one month after the payments are made, one of the spouses moves; and
4. There is no liability to make any payments for any period after the death of the payee-spouse and there is no liability to make substitute payments (in cash or property) after the death of the payee-spouse. If the divorce decree fails to state that the payments cease when the payee-spouse dies neither the payments made before or after the death of the payee-spouse qualified as deductible alimony.

The term "divorce or separation instrument" is defined as:

1. A final decree of divorce or separate maintenance or a written instrument incident to such a decree;
2. A written separation agreement (oral separation agreement will not qualify). A written separation agreement has been interpreted to require a clear, written statement memorializing the terms of support between the parties and entered into in contemplation of separation status; or
3. A decree or temporary support order requiring a spouse to make payments for the support or maintenance of the other spouse. Payments made before the existence of a written divorce or separation instrument were not considered alimony for tax purposes.

A child support payment is a payment that the terms of the divorce or separation instrument fix as a sum payable for the support of children of the payor-spouse. Child support payments will not be treated as alimony and therefore were not deductible by the payor-spouse and were not treated as income by the recipient-spouse. An amount specified in a divorce or separation instrument is treated as a fixed payment made for child support (and therefore was not deductible as alimony) to the extent the amount is to be reduced either:

1. When a contingency, specified in the instrument, relating to a child or payor occurs; or
2. At a time that can clearly be associated with such a contingency.

Alimony Deduction and Exclusion Repealed. The new law provides that for any divorce or separation agreement executed after December 31, 2018, or executed before that date but modified after it (if the modification expressly provides that the new amendments apply), alimony and separate maintenance payments are not deductible by the payor-spouse and are not included in the income of the payee-spouse. Instead, income used for alimony payments is taxed at the rates applicable to the payor-spouse rather than the recipient-spouse. The new law does not change the tax treatment of child support payments.

> **Practical Tip:** If you are in the middle of divorce proceedings where you will be required to pay alimony, be sure to execute the divorce or separation agreement prior to December 31, 2018 to preserve the deductibility of the alimony and/or separate maintenance payments by the *payor-spouse.* If you are the *payee-spouse,* you would want the agreement to be executed *after* December 31, 2018 so that the alimony and/or separate maintenance payments would not be included in your income.

§ 4.10 Deduction for Moving Expenses

When taxpayers make a work-related move, were previously able to deduct qualified "moving expenses" paid or incurred during the tax year in connection with commencement of work at a new job. The deduction was available to both employees and self-employed taxpayers. Self-employed individuals are treated as having obtained employment when they make substantial arrangements to commence work in the new location (*e.g.,* lease or purchase workspace and equipment, make arrangements to purchase inventory and make arrangements to contact customers).

Under the old law, taxpayers could claim a deduction for moving expenses incurred in connection with starting a new job if the new workplace was at least 50 miles farther from a taxpayer's former residence than the former place of work. To qualify for the deduction, the following three requirements must have been satisfied:

1. The taxpayer's moving expenses must have been paid or incurred by the taxpayer in connection with his "commencement" of work at a new "principal place of work;"
2. The taxpayer have satisfied the "distance test;" and
3. The taxpayer have satisfied the "time test."

The term "commencement" of work included:

1. The beginning of work by a taxpayer as an employee or as a self-employed individual for the first time or after a substantial period of unemployment or part-time employment;
2. The beginning of work by a taxpayer for a different employer or, in the case of a self-employed individual, in a new trade or business; or
3. The beginning of work by a taxpayer for the same employer or, in the case of a self-employed individual, in the same trade or business at a new location.

To qualify as being in connection with the commencement of work, the move must bear a reasonable proximity both in time and place to such commencement at the new principal place of work. In general, moving expenses incurred within one year of the date of the commencement of work were considered to be reasonably proximate in time to such commencement.

Under previous law, moving expenses incurred after the one-year period were considered reasonably proximate in time if it could be shown that circumstances existed which prevented the taxpayer from incurring the expenses of moving within the one-year period allowed. Whether circumstances existed which prevented the taxpayer from incurring the expenses of moving within the period allowed was dependent upon the facts and circumstances of each case. The length of the delay and the fact that the taxpayer may have incurred part of the expenses of the move within the one-year period allowed was taken into account in determining whether expenses incurred after such period were allowable.

In general, a move is not considered to be reasonably proximate in place to the commencement of work at the new principal place of work where the distance between the taxpayer's new residence and his new principal place of work exceeds the distance between his former residence and his new principal place of work. A move to a new residence which does not satisfy this test may, however, be considered reasonably proximate in place to the commencement of work if the taxpayer can demonstrate, for example, that he is required to live at such residence as a condition of employment or that living at such residence will result in an actual decrease in commuting time or expense.

A taxpayer's "principal place of work" is usually the place where he spends the greater portion of his working time. An employee's principal place of work is generally his employer's plant, office, shop, store, or other property. If a taxpayer does not spend a substantial portion of his time at any one place, his principal place of work is that place where his business activities are centered. For example, the principal place of work of a railroad conductor, who spends most of his or her time aboard a train, is his or her home terminal, station, or other central point where he or she reports in, checks out, or receives instructions.

Taxpayers are divided into two groups for satisfying the minimum distance requirement:

1. Taxpayers who have a former principal place of work including those who are reentering the work force after a substantial period of unemployment or part-time employment; and
2. Taxpayers who did not have a former principal place of work including individuals who are seeking full-time employment for the first time (*e.g.,* recent graduates).

In the case of a taxpayer having a former principal place of work, under prior law, no deduction was allowed unless the distance between the former residence and the new principal place of work exceeded by at least 50 miles the distance between the former residence and the former principal place of work. Note that there was no requirement that his old and new homes be at least 50 miles apart. For example, if the distance between a taxpayer's old residence and the former place of employment was 10 miles, the location of the new place of employment must be at least 60 miles from the old residence.

In the case of a taxpayer not having a former principal place of work, no deduction was allowed unless the distance between the former residence and the new principal place of work was at least 50 miles.

For purposes of measuring distances, the distance between two geographic points is measured by the shortest of the more commonly traveled routes between such points. The shortest of the more commonly traveled routes refers to the line of travel and the mode or modes of transportation commonly used to go between two geographic points comprising the shortest distance between such points irrespective of the route used by the taxpayer.

Under prior law, in order for the taxpayer to deduct his or her moving expenses, the taxpayer must also have satisfied the "time test" which requires the taxpayer to work in the new locale for a specific length of time. Different time requirements apply to employees and self-employed taxpayers as discussed below. To have been eligible for a deduction, employees must have worked full-time for at least 39 weeks during the 12-month period immediately following the start of work in the new location. The time is measured from the arrival date in the new job's general location.

It was not necessary for the employee to remain employed by the same employer for the 39-week period. The employee must, however, count only full-time employment. To be eligible for the moving expense deduction, the employee must have been employed in the same general location of the new job.

A taxpayer-employee must have met the 39-week test regardless of whether he was reimbursed for his moving expenses. The 39-week test was waived only if the taxpayer's failure to meet it was due to death, disability, or involuntary separation (other than for willful misconduct) from the service of, or transfer for the benefit of, an employer after obtaining full-time employment in which he could reasonably have been expected to satisfy the 39-week requirement.

The 12-month period was measured from the date the taxpayer-employee arrived in the new general location in which he will be working, whether his family arrived then or later. In making the 39-week computation, only weeks in which the taxpayer was a full-time employee were counted. Whether or not the taxpayer was a full-time employee was gauged by the customs of the trade in the locality to which he moved. For taxpayers engaged in seasonal occupations, the off-season was counted only if: (1) it was covered by the taxpayer's employment contract, and (2) it was *less* than six months. Thus, a schoolteacher whose employment contract covered a 12-month period and who taught on a full-time basis for more than six months in fulfillment of such contract was considered to be a full-time employee during the entire 12-month period. A taxpayer would not be considered as other than a full-time employee during any week merely because of periods of involuntary temporary absence from work because of illness, strikes, shutouts, layoffs, natural disaster, etc.

If taxpayers filed a joint return, either spouse was able to satisfy the 39-week requirement. However, weeks worked by one spouse could not be added to weeks worked by the other spouse in order to satisfy the 39-week requirement.

The "self-employed individual" was defined for purposes of the moving expense deduction as an individual who performed personal services either as the owner of the entire interest in an unincorporated trade or business or as a partner in a partnership carrying on a trade or business. In general, the term "self-employed individual" does not include the semi-retired, part-time students, or other similarly situated taxpayers who work only a few hours each week. Self-employed individuals are treated as having obtained employment when they make substantial arrangements to commence work in the new location. This would include leasing or purchasing workspace and equipment, making arrangements to purchase inventory and making arrangements to contact clients or customers). Moving expenses incurred for such a taxpayer after the one-year period were likely deductible if the taxpayer could show that circumstances prevented the taxpayer from incurring the expenses of moving within the one-year period. Although the facts and circumstances may vary, the length of the delay and the fact that the taxpayer may have incurred part of the moving expenses within the one-year period were taken into account.

A self-employed taxpayer must have worked full time for at least 39 weeks during the first year and for a total of at least 78 weeks during the first two years after arriving in the area of the new workplace. If spouses that file a joint return both work full time, either of the spouses were able to satisfy the full-time work test. If either of the spouses failed to satisfy the time test, the couple could not combine the weeks that they each individually worked to satisfy it.

Only the following reasonable moving expenses were deductible:

1. The cost of moving household goods, furnishings and personal effects from the former residence to the new residence;
2. The cost of packing, crating and in-transit storage and insurance for such goods;
3. The cost of connecting and disconnecting utilities; and
4. The cost of traveling, including lodging during the period of travel from the former residence to the new residence.

The moving expenses of "members of the taxpayer's household" were also deductible if such persons resided with the taxpayer before and after the move. For the expenses of members of the taxpayer's household to be deductible, it was not necessary that all members of the household travel together or at the same time. The deduction for "members of the taxpayer's household" excluded a tenant residing in the residence, or a person who was an employee of the taxpayer such as a governess, chauffeur, nurse, valet, or personal attendant.

New Tax Law Suspends Moving Expense Deduction Except in Limited Situations. The new law provides that for tax years beginning after

December 31, 2017 and before January 1, 2026, the deduction for moving expenses is suspended, except for members of the Armed Forces (or their spouse or dependents) on active duty who move pursuant to a military order and incident to a permanent change of station.

> **Comment.** The new law suspends the deduction for moving expenses after 2017 (except for certain members of the Armed Forces), and also suspends the tax-free reimbursement of employment-related moving expenses. Therefore, if you are in the middle of a job-related move, you should try and request a reimbursement from an employer. Note, however, that after 2017, that reimbursement for moving expenses from your employer will be treated as income, and you will pay income tax on it.

§ 4.11 Deduction of Employee Business Entertainment Expenses

Under prior law, a taxpayer could not claim a deduction for expenses associated with the following:

1. An activity generally considered to be entertainment, amusement, or recreation unless the taxpayer established that the item was directly related to or associated with the active conduct of the taxpayer's trade or business, or
2. A facility (*e.g.*, an airplane) used in connection with such activity.

If the taxpayer established that entertainment expenses were directly related to or associated with the active conduct of its trade or business, the deduction generally was limited to 50% of the amount otherwise deductible. Similarly, a deduction for any expense for food or beverages generally was limited to 50% of the amount otherwise deductible. In addition, no deduction was allowed for membership dues with respect to any club organized for business, pleasure, recreation, or other social purpose.

There were a number of exceptions to the general rule disallowing deduction of entertainment expenses and the rules limiting deductions to 50% of the otherwise deductible amount. Under one such exception, those rules did not apply to expenses for goods, services, and facilities to the extent that the expenses were reported by the taxpayer as compensation and as wages to an employee. Those rules also did not apply to expenses for goods, services, and facilities to the extent that the expenses were includible in the gross income of a recipient who was not an employee (*e.g.*, a nonemployee director) as compensation for services rendered or as a prize or award. The exceptions applied only to the extent that amounts were properly reported by the company as compensation and wages or otherwise includible in income. In no event could the amount of the deduction exceed the amount of the taxpayer's actual cost, even if a greater amount (*i.e.,* fair market value) was includible in income.

Those deduction disallowance rules also did not apply to expenses paid or incurred by the taxpayer, in connection with the performance of services for another person (other than an employer), under a reimbursement or other expense allowance arrangement if the taxpayer accounted for the expenses to such person. Another exception applied for expenses for recreational, social, or similar activities primarily for the benefit of employees other than certain owners and highly-compensated employees. An exception applied also to the 50% deduction limit for food and beverages provided to crew members of certain commercial vessels and certain oil or gas platform or drilling rig workers.

A taxpayer was able to deduct up to 50% of expenses relating to meals and entertainment. Housing and meals provided for the convenience of the employer on the business premises of the employer were excluded from the employee's gross income. Various other fringe benefits provided by employers were not included in an employee's gross income, such as qualified transportation fringe benefits.

New Law Eliminates Deductions for Some Entertainment, Meal and Transportation Expenses. The new law provides that effective for amounts incurred or paid after December 31, 2017, no deduction will be allowed for:

1. An activity generally considered to be entertainment, amusement or recreation;
2. Membership dues paid to any club organized for business, pleasure, recreation or other social purposes; or
3. A facility or any portion of a facility used in connection with entertainment, amusement or recreation.

Therefore, the new law repeals the exception to the deduction disallowance for entertainment, amusement, or recreation that is directly related to the active conduct of the taxpayer's trade or business. The new law also repeals the related rule applying a 50% limit to such deductions.

> **Comment.** Some entertainment-related rules do not change. As under current law, club dues and membership costs are not deductible and when entertainment deductions are disallowed with respect to

any portion of a facility, that portion is treated as a personal, rather than a business asset.

Some entertainment expenses also remain fully deductible, including: (a) certain entertainment expenses for goods, services, and facilities that are treated as compensation to an employee-recipient; (b) expenses for recreational, social, or similar activities and related facilities primarily for the benefit of employees who are not highly-compensated employees; (c) expenses for entertainment sold to customers; and (d) entertainment expenses for goods, services, and facilities that are includible in the gross income of a non-employee recipient as compensation for services rendered or as a prize or award. As under prior law, these deductions must satisfy strict substantiation requirements; however, the taxpayer will not have to substantiate the time and place of the entertainment.

Taxpayers may still generally deduct 50% of the food and beverage expenses associated with operating their trade or business. For example, employers may deduct expenses incurred to provide meals consumed by employees on work travel. For amounts incurred and paid after December 31, 2017 and before December 31, 2025, the new law expands the 50% limit on the deductibility of business meals to include expenses associated with meals provided for the convenience of the employer on the employer's business premises, or provided on or near the employer's business premises through an employer-operated facility that meets certain requirements.

Comment. An employer may continue to deduct 50% of its expenses for food, beverages, and related facilities that are furnished on its business premises primarily for its employees, such as in a typical company cafeteria or executive dining room.

§ 4.12 Miscellaneous Itemized Deductions

An individual taxpayer was formerly able to claim itemized deductions for certain miscellaneous itemized deductions to the extent that the taxpayer's total miscellaneous expenses exceeded 2% of the taxpayer's AGI. Individual taxpayers could deduct all ordinary and necessary expenses paid or incurred during the tax year for the production or collection of income. The following list gives examples of expenses that qualified and therefore could be deducted under this provision:

1. Appraisal fees for a casualty loss or charitable contribution;
2. Casualty and theft losses from property used in performing services as an employee;
3. Clerical help and office rent in caring for investments;
4. Depreciation on home computers used for investments;
5. Excess deductions including administrative expenses allowed a beneficiary on termination of an estate or trust;
6. Fees to collect interest and dividends;
7. Indirect miscellaneous deductions from pass-through entities;
8. Investment fees and expenses;
9. Loss on deposits in an insolvent or bankrupt financial institution;
10. Loss on traditional IRAs or Roth IRAs, when all amounts have been distributed;
11. Repayments of income;
12. Safe deposit box rental fees;
13. Service charges on dividend reinvestment plans;
14. Trustee's fees for an IRA, if separately billed and paid;
15. Expenses incurred for management of undeveloped land and other property held for appreciation;
16. Fees to collect interest and dividends;
17. Hobby expenses, but generally not more than hobby income. Note that the hobby income limitation is applied before the 2% rule;
18. Liquidated damages paid to a former employer for breach of an employment contract;
19. Expenses of looking for a new job (including fees paid to employment agencies and resume printing and mailing costs);
20. Employee's malpractice insurance premiums;
21. Medical examinations required by an employer;
22. Occupational taxes;
23. Research expenses of a college professor;
24. User fee paid to the IRS for ruling requests;
25. Travel expenses incurred in connection with managing the taxpayer's investments; and
26. Wrap fees paid on brokerage accounts that charge a flat percentage fee instead of a commission.

Tax Preparation Expenses. Also qualifying, under prior law, as miscellaneous expenses are the expenses that individual taxpayers incurred for tax preparation and other tax-related services such as tax counsel fees and appraisal fees.

Unreimbursed Employee Business Expenses. Employees were also able to claim a miscellaneous expense deduction for their unreimbursed trade or business expenses but only to the extent that the expenses exceeded 2% of the employee's adjusted gross income. Examples of unreimbursed expenses attributable to the trade or business of being an employee include the following:

1. Business bad debt of an employee;
2. Business liability insurance premiums;
3. Damages paid to a former employer for breach of an employment contract;
4. Depreciation on a computer a taxpayer's employer requires him to use in his work;
5. Dues to a chamber of commerce if membership helped the taxpayer perform his job;
6. Dues to professional societies;
7. Educator expenses;
8. Home office or part of a taxpayer's home used regularly and exclusively in the taxpayer's work;
9. Job search expenses in the taxpayer's present occupation;
10. Laboratory breakage fees;
11. Legal fees related to the taxpayer's job;
12. Licenses and regulatory fees;
13. Malpractice insurance premiums;
14. Medical examinations required by an employer;
15. Occupational taxes;
16. Passport fees for a business trip;
17. Repayment of an income aid payment received under an employer's plan;
18. Research expenses of a college professor;
19. Rural mail carriers' vehicle expenses;
20. Subscriptions to professional journals and trade magazines related to the taxpayer's work;
21. Tools and supplies used in the taxpayer's work;
22. Purchase of travel, transportation, meals, entertainment, gifts, and local lodging related to the taxpayer's work;
23. Union dues and expenses;
24. Work clothes and uniforms, if required, and not suitable for everyday use; and
25. Work-related education.

Other miscellaneous itemized deductions subject to the 2% floor included:

1. Repayments of income received under a claim of right (only subject to the 2% floor if less than $3,000);
2. Repayments of Social Security benefits; and
3. The share of deductible investment expenses from pass-through entities.

New Tax Law Suspends Deduction of Miscellaneous Itemized Deductions. For tax years beginning after December 31, 2017 and before January 1, 2026, the deduction for miscellaneous itemized deductions that are subject to the 2% floor is suspended. Therefore, no miscellaneous itemized deductions may be claimed by an individual on Schedule A of Form 1040 for tax years 2018 through 2025.

CHAPTER 5

Exclusions from Gross Income

§ 5.01 Exclusion for Employee Achievement Awards

An employee's gross income does not include the value of achievement awards received by the employee for length of service or safety achievement. The term "employee achievement award" means an item of "tangible personal property" which is (1) transferred by an employer to an employee for length of service achievement or safety achievement; (2) awarded as part of a meaningful presentation; and (3) awarded under conditions and circumstances that do not create a significant likelihood of the payment of disguised compensation.

The exclusion is not available for awards of cash, gift certificates or similar items such as vacations, meals, lodging, tickets to theatre or sporting events, stocks, bonds, and other securities.

For purposes of this exclusion, the following individuals qualify as employees: (1) a current employee; (2) a former common-law employee that the employer provided coverage for in consideration of or based on an agreement relating to prior services as an employee; and (3) a leased employee who has provided services to the employer on a substantially full-time basis for at least a year, if the services are performed under the employer's primary direction or control.

The exclusion is generally limited to awards that cost an employer $400 per employee per year. However, the ceiling is $1,600 per employee per year for a qualified plan award. A qualified plan award is one made under an established written plan that does not discriminate in favor of "highly-compensated employees." A "highly-compensated employee" is defined as an employee (1) who was a 5% owner at any time during the year or the preceding year or (2) who was paid more than $120,000 in 2017. The $1,600 ceiling is the overall limit when an employee is given both qualified and nonqualified plan awards during the year. As a result, the $400 and the $1,600 maximums cannot be added together in one year.

An award will not qualify for the exclusion if it is received within the employee's first five years of employment or if the employee received a similar award during the current year or the preceding four years. An award will not be considered an excludable safety achievement award if employee safety achievement awards were granted during the year to more than 10% of the employer's employees (excluding managers, administrators, clerical employees and other professional employees) or were granted at all to a manager, administrator, clerical employee or other professional employee.

New Law Says that Cash, Gift Cards and Other Property Don't Qualify as Employee Achievement Awards. For amounts paid or incurred after December 31, 2017, the new law revises the definition of "tangible personal property" to provide that "tangible personal property" does not include cash, cash equivalents, gifts cards, gift coupons, gift certificates (other than arrangements conferring only the right to select and receive tangible personal property from a limited array of such items pre-selected or pre-arranged by the employer) or vacations, meals, lodging, tickets to the theater or sporting events, stocks, bonds or other securities or similar items. No inference is intended that this is a change from present law and guidance.

§ 5.02 Exclusion for Qualified Moving Expense Reimbursements

Qualified moving expense reimbursements are defined as any amount received either directly or indirectly by an employee from an employer as payment for, or a reimbursement of expenses that would be deductible as moving expenses if directly paid or incurred by the employee. Formerly, an employee could exclude qualified moving expense reimbursements from his or her gross income for income tax purposes and from his or her wages for employment tax purposes.

New Tax Law Suspends Exclusion for Moving Expense Reimbursements Paid by Employers. For tax years beginning after December 31, 2017 and before January 1, 2026, the exclusion for qualified moving expense reimbursements is suspended, except for members of the Armed Forces on active duty (and their spouses and dependents) who move pursuant to a military order and incident to a permanent change of station.

§ 5.03 Exclusion for Qualified Transportation Fringe Benefits

Under prior law, an employee could exclude from his or her gross income up to $20 per month in qualified bicycle commuting reimbursements.

Qualified reimbursements were any amount received from an employer during a 15-month period beginning with the first day of the calendar year as payment for reasonable expenses during a calendar year. Reasonable expenses were those incurred in a calendar year for the purchase of a bicycle and bicycle improvements, repair and storage, if the bicycle was regularly used for travel between the employee's residence and place of employment. Amounts that were excludable from gross income for income tax purposes were also excluded from wages for employment tax purposes.

New Law Suspends Exclusion for Bicycle Commuting Reimbursements. For tax years beginning after December 31, 2017 and before January 1, 2026, the exclusion from gross income and wages for qualified bicycle commuting reimbursements is suspended.

Practical Tip: The exclusions for reimbursements of parking, mass transit, and van pool reimbursements have not been suspended, so if these programs are available from your employer, you may want to leave your bike in the garage and catch a train.

CHAPTER 6

Retirement Plans and IRAs

§ 6.01 Recharacterization of Roth IRA Contributions

If an individual makes a contribution to an individual retirement account (IRA) (traditional or Roth) for a tax year, the individual is allowed to recharacterize the contribution as a contribution to the other type of IRA (traditional or Roth) by making a trustee-to-trustee transfer to the other type of IRA before the due date for the individual's income tax return for that year. In the case of a recharacterization, the contribution will be treated as having been made to the transferee IRA (and not the original, transferor IRA) as of the date of the original contribution. Formerly, both regular contributions and conversion contributions to a Roth IRA could be recharacterized as having been made to a traditional IRA.

For tax years beginning after December 31, 2017, the new law repeals the special rule that allows IRA contributions to one type of IRA (either traditional or Roth) to be recharacterized as a contribution to the other type of IRA. For example, a conversion contribution establishing a Roth IRA during a tax year can no longer be recharacterized as a contribution to a traditional IRA which in effect results in unwinding the conversion.

Recharacterization is still permitted in other situations. For example, an individual can still make a contribution for a year to a Roth IRA and before the due date for the individual's income tax return for that year, recharacterize it as a contribution to a traditional IRA. In essence, recharacterization provisions can no longer be used to unwind a Roth conversion.

Caution. An individual may still make a contribution for a year to a Roth IRA and, before the due date for the individual's income tax return for that year, recharacterize it as a contribution to a traditional IRA. In addition, an individual may still make a contribution to a traditional IRA and convert the traditional IRA to a Roth IRA, but the individual is precluded from later unwinding the conversion through a recharacterization.

The strategy behind recharacterizing a conversion hinged on changes in the market price of the IRA assets during the course of the year. The owner pays tax in a conversion based on the value of the assets on the conversion date, so the tax liability is locked in on that date. If the value of the assets goes up significantly, the conversion looks like a shrewd move because the tax bill would have been higher if the taxpayer had waited. If, instead, the value goes down (e.g., through a market correction or through recession), the conversion looks like a foolish mistake because the tax bill is much higher than if the owner had waited until the asset prices fell. The option to recharacterize (no longer available) reduced this risk.

§ 6.02 Retirement Plan Loans

Employees who participate in their employer's retirement plan may borrow money from those plans if the employer's retirement plan is either: (1) a qualified plan that satisfies the requirements of the Code; (2) an annuity plan that satisfies the requirements of the Code; or (3) a governmental plan. Loans are *not* permitted from IRAs or from IRA-based plans such as SEPs, SARSEPs and SIMPLE IRA plans. If the owner of an IRA borrows from the IRA, the IRA is no longer considered an IRA, and the value of the entire IRA is included in the owner's income.

If the employee's plan allows plan loans, the employee must complete loan forms and sign a repayment agreement outlining the number, the amount, and the due dates of repayment. A loan must be evidenced by a legally enforceable agreement. However, the agreement need not be signed in jurisdictions where a signature is not required for the loan to be enforceable. The employees must pay interest on the amount borrowed and, depending upon the terms for loans as stated in the plan, may have to agree to repay the loan using automatic deductions from their future wages. If a participant failed to make payments on a plan loan, the missed payments can still be made even after a deemed distribution has occurred.

A loan to a participant in a qualified employer plan will not be treated as a deemed (taxable) distribution if it satisfies the following requirements:

1. The plan loan must be repaid within five years. If the terms of the loan call for a payment period of more than five years, the entire loan

is considered a taxable distribution, even if the loan is actually paid off within five years. If, however, a five-year loan is not paid off within the required period, only the outstanding balance at that time is considered a taxable distribution. The five-year repayment requirement does not apply to loans used to acquire the plan participant's principal residence. A loan that is taken for the purpose of purchasing the employee's principal residence may be paid back over a period of more than five years. Note that taking a loan to cover the cost of refinancing does not qualify as a principal residence plan loan. A plan may suspend loan repayments for employees performing military service. A plan may also suspend loan repayments during a leave of absence of up to one year. However, upon return, the participant must make up the missed payments either by increasing the amount of each monthly payment or by paying a lump sum at the end, so that the term of the loan does not exceed the original five-year term.

2. The loan repayments must be substantially equal and must be made at least quarterly. The terms of repayment must be level amortization. This means that making a balloon payment at the end of five years will not work.

3. The loan amount cannot exceed the lesser of:
    a. $50,000, or
    b. One-half of the present value of the employee's vested benefits under the plan.

4. The plan loan must be evidenced by a legally enforceable written agreement with terms that (a) demonstrate compliance with the requirements for non-distribution treatment, (b) specify the amount and date of the loan, and (c) outline the repayment schedule.

If the plan loan fails to satisfy the requirements outlined above regarding the amount, duration and repayment of the loan, the loan proceeds will be treated as a deemed distribution includible in taxable income and potentially subject to a 10% premature distribution penalty.

In addition, the following requirements must be satisfied to avoid any tax consequences:

1. All plan participants (active and inactive employees) must be able to borrow money from their retirement account on a reasonably equivalent basis. A plan can only make distinctions based on creditworthiness and financial need;

2. Loans cannot be made to highly-compensated employees in an amount greater than what is available to other employees. Highly-compensated

employees include sole proprietors, partners owning more than 10% of the capital or profits interest in a partnership, and an employee or officer of a subchapter C corporation owning more than 5% of the outstanding stock of the corporation;

3. The plan must specifically set forth the terms under which loans will be made;

4. The debt must be adequately secured; and

5. The plan must charge a reasonable rate of interest. The plan must be able to foreclose on the collateral in the event of a default, and the value of the collateral must be sufficient so that the plan will not suffer any loss of principal or interest between the date of default and the date of the foreclosure on the collateral.

A deemed distribution is treated as an actual distribution for purposes of determining the tax on the distribution, including the penalty that may apply. A deemed distribution is also subject to withholding and information reporting.

If an employee stops making payments on a retirement plan loan before the loan is repaid, the employee has defaulted on the loan and a deemed distribution of the outstanding loan balance generally occurs. Such a distribution is generally taxed as though an actual distribution occurred, including being subject to a 10% premature penalty tax. Note that if you are over age 59½ you may not be subject to the premature penalty tax. A deemed distribution is not eligible for rollover to another eligible retirement plan.

A plan may also provide that, in certain circumstances (for example, if an employee terminates employment), an employee's obligation to repay a loan is accelerated and, if the loan is not repaid, the loan is cancelled and the amount in the employee's account balance is offset by the amount of the unpaid loan balance, referred to as a loan offset. A loan offset is treated as an actual distribution from the plan equal to the unpaid loan balance (rather than a deemed distribution), and, unlike a deemed distribution, the amount of the distribution is eligible for a tax-free rollover to another eligible retirement plan within 60 days. However, the plan is not required to offer a direct rollover with respect to a plan loan offset amount that is an eligible rollover distribution, and the plan loan offset amount is generally not subject to a 20% income tax withholding.

New Law Gives Employees Extra Time to Roll Over Plan Loan Offsets. For plan loan offset amounts which are treated as distributed in tax years beginning after December 31, 2017, the new law provides that the period during which a qualified plan loan offset amount may be contributed to an eligible retirement plan as a rollover contribution is extended from 60 days after the date of the offset to the due date (including extensions) for filing the federal income tax return for the tax year in which the plan loan offset occurs—that is, the tax year in which the amount is treated as distributed from the plan.

A qualified plan loan offset amount is a plan loan offset amount that is treated as distributed from a qualified retirement plan, a Code Sec. 403(b) plan, or a governmental plan solely by reason of the termination of the plan or the failure to meet the repayment terms of the loan because of the employee's separation from service, whether due to layoff, cessation of business, termination of employment, or otherwise. A loan offset amount under the Act (as before) is the amount by which an employee's account balance under the plan is reduced to repay a loan from the plan.

§ 6.03 Retirement Fund Distributions for 2016 Disaster Areas

An individual who receives an early distribution from a qualified retirement plan, a tax-sheltered annuity plan, an eligible deferred compensation plan of a state or local government employer, or an IRA generally must include the distribution in income for the year distributed. In addition, unless an exception applies, a distribution from a qualified retirement plan, a Code Sec. 403(b) plan or an IRA received before the individual has reached age 59½ is subject to a 10% additional tax (the "early withdrawal tax") on the amount includible in income.

In general, a distribution from an eligible retirement plan may be rolled over to another eligible retirement plan within 60 days, in which case the amount rolled over generally is not includible in income. The IRS has the authority to waive the 60-day rollover requirement if failure to waive the requirement would be against equity or good conscience, including in cases of casualty, disaster or other events beyond the reasonable control of the individual.

New Law Provides Relief for Qualified 2016 Disaster Distributions Relief. The new law provides an exception to the retirement plan 10% early withdrawal tax for up to $100,000 of "qualified 2016 disaster distributions." These distributions are defined as distributions from an eligible retirement plan made (a) on or after January 1, 2016 and before January 1, 2018, to an individual whose principal place of abode at any time during 2016 was located in a 2016 disaster area and who has sustained an economic loss by reason of the events that gave rise to the federal disaster declaration.

An "eligible retirement plan" means a qualified retirement plan, a Code Sec. 403(b) plan or an IRA. Income attributable to a qualified 2016 disaster distribution can, under the Act, be included in income ratably over three years and the amount of a qualified 2016 disaster distribution can be recontributed to an eligible retirement plan within three years.

The new law also provides that a plan amendment made pursuant to the above disaster relief provisions may be retroactively effective if certain requirements are met, including that it be made on or before the last day of the first plan year beginning after December 31, 2018 (December 31, 2020 for a governmental plan), or a later date prescribed by the IRS.

> **Practical Tip:** Earlier in 2017, Congress provided disaster distributions relief in response to Hurricanes Harvey, Irma, and Maria, but limited relief only to those people affected by those storms. This new provision extends relief to any individuals affected by any federally declared disaster in 2016 or 2017; not just hurricanes, but also wildfires, floods, winter storms or other declared disaster.

§ 6.04 Deferred Compensation of *Bona Fide* Public Safety Volunteers

Employees of a state or local government or a tax-exempt organization are not currently taxed for compensation deferred under an eligible deferred compensation plan if the plan satisfies participation, deferral, payout, trust, and other requirements. There are a number of plans to which these rules do not apply.

Plans that pay length-of-service awards to *bona fide* safety volunteers or to their beneficiaries on account of fire-fighting and prevention services, emergency medical services, or ambulance services performed by the volunteers are not subject to the requirements for unfunded deferred compensation plans with respect to awards accrued after 1996. A *bona fide* volunteer is an individual who does not receive any compensation for performing the qualified services other than (1) reimbursements or reasonable allowances for expenses incurred in performing the services, or (2) benefits and nominal fees for performing the services that are reasonable and customarily paid by tax-exempt and governmental employers for such services. A length-of-service award plan will not qualify for this treatment if the total amount of awards accrued for any year of service of any volunteer exceeds $3,000.

New Law Doubles Accrued Benefit Limit for *Bona Fide* Public Safety Volunteers. Effective for tax years beginning after December 31, 2017, the new law increases the aggregate amount of length of service awards that may accrue for a *bona fide* volunteer with respect to any year of service to $6,000 and adjusts that amount in $500 increments to reflect changes in cost-of-living for years after the first year the provision is effective. In addition, under the provision, if the plan is a defined benefit plan, the limit applies to the actuarial present value of the aggregate amount of length of service awards accruing with respect to any year of service.

Actuarial present value is to be calculated using reasonable actuarial assumptions and methods, assuming payment will be made under the most valuable form of payment under the plan with payment commencing at the later of the earliest age at which unreduced benefits are payable under the plan or the participant's age at the time of the calculation.

> **Practical Tip.** You can still impact your 2017 taxes by making a 2017 IRA contribution (up to $5,500 per individual with catch-up contributions of an additional $1,000 if you are age 50 or older) before April 17, 2018.

CHAPTER 7

Estate, Gift and Generation-Skipping Transfer Tax

§ 7.01 Overview of Estate, Gift and Generation-Skipping Transfer Taxes
§ 7.02 Effect of the Tax Cuts and Jobs Act on the Unified Credit for Federal Estate, Gift and GST Taxes

§ 7.01 Overview of Estate, Gift and Generation-Skipping Transfer Taxes

Individual taxpayers are subject to a gift tax on lifetime transfers, an estate tax on certain transfers at death, and a generation-skipping transfer (GST) tax on transfers either directly or through a trust or similar arrangement, to a "skip person" (*i.e.*, a beneficiary in a generation more than one generation younger than that of the transferor). Transfers subject to the generation-skipping transfer tax include direct skips, taxable terminations, and taxable distributions.

Estate Tax. An estate tax is imposed on the transfer of the taxable estate of every decedent who is a citizen or resident of the United States and generally is based on the fair market value of the property passing at death. The taxable estate generally equals the worldwide gross estate less certain allowable deductions, including a marital deduction for certain bequests to the surviving spouse of the decedent and a deduction for certain bequests to charities.

A decedent's gross estate includes the date-of-death value of all of a decedent's property, real or personal, tangible or intangible, wherever situated. In general, the value of property for this purpose is the fair market value of the property as of the date of the decedent's death, although an executor may elect to value certain property as of the date that is six months after the decedent's death (the alternate valuation date).

The gross estate includes not only property directly owned by the decedent, but also other property in which the decedent had a beneficial interest at the time of his or her death. The gross estate also includes certain transfers made by the decedent prior to his or her death, including: (1) certain gifts made within three years prior to the decedent's death; (2) certain transfers of property in which the decedent retained a life estate; (3) certain transfers taking effect at death; and (4) revocable transfers. In addition, the decedent's gross estate also includes property over which the decedent had, at the time of death, a general power of appointment (generally, the right to determine who will have beneficial ownership). The value of a life insurance policy on the decedent's life is included in the gross estate if the proceeds are payable to the decedent's estate or the decedent had incidents of ownership with respect to the policy at the time of his or her death.

Gift Tax. A gift tax is imposed on the transfer of property by gift during such year by any individual, whether a resident or nonresident of the United States. The amount of a taxpayer's taxable gifts for a calendar year is determined by subtracting from the total amount of gifts made during the year: (1) the gift tax annual exclusion; and (2) allowable deductions.

Gift tax for the current taxable year is determined by: (1) computing a tentative tax on the combined amount of all taxable gifts for the current and all prior calendar years using the common gift tax and estate tax rate table; (2) computing a tentative tax only on all prior-year gifts; (3) subtracting the tentative tax on prior-year gifts from the tentative tax computed for all years to arrive at the portion of the total tentative tax attributable to current-year gifts; and, finally, (4) subtracting the amount of unified credit not consumed by prior-year gifts.

The gift tax applies to a transfer by gift regardless of whether: (1) the transfer is made outright or in trust; (2) the gift is direct or indirect; or (3) the property is real or personal, tangible or intangible. For gift tax purposes, the value of a gift of property is the fair market value of the property at the time of the gift. Where property is transferred for less than full consideration, the amount by which the value of the property exceeds the value of the consideration is considered a gift and is included in computing the total amount of a taxpayer's gifts for a calendar year.

For a gift to occur, a donor generally must relinquish dominion and control over donated property. For example, if a taxpayer transfers assets to a trust established for the benefit of his or her children, but retains the right to revoke the trust, the taxpayer may not have made a completed gift, because the taxpayer has retained dominion and control over the transferred assets. A completed gift made in trust, on the other hand, is often treated as a gift to the trust beneficiaries.

Gift Tax Annual Exclusion. Donors of lifetime gifts are provided an annual gift tax exclusion in the amount of $15,000 to an unlimited number of donees in 2018 for gifts of present interests in property during the taxable year. If not used in 2018, the annual gift tax exclusion is lost and cannot accumulate from year to year. The annual gift tax exclusion is only available for gifts of a "present interest" in property. A present interest is a legal term which means that the enjoyment or possession of the gift must be immediate or in the present rather than off in the distant future. Gifts of "future interests," which are defined as gifts where possession or enjoyment of the property is postponed until some future time such as after someone else dies (as is the case with a remainder interest in a trust) do not generally qualify for the gift tax exclusion unless special requirements are met.

If the non-donor spouse consents to split the gift with the donor spouse, then the annual exclusion is $30,000 per donee in 2018. In general, unlimited transfers between spouses are permitted without imposition of a gift tax. Special rules apply to the contributions to a qualified tuition program ("529 Plan") including an election to treat a contribution that exceeds the annual exclusion as a contribution made ratably over a five-year period beginning with the year of the contribution.

Generation-Skipping Transfer Tax. The generation-skipping transfer tax is a separate tax that can be imposed (in addition to the gift tax or the estate tax) on transfers, either directly or in trust or similar arrangement, to a "skip person" (*i.e.*, a beneficiary in a generation more than one generation below that of the transferor). Transfers subject to the generation-skipping transfer tax include direct skips, taxable terminations, and taxable distributions.

A direct skip is any transfer subject to estate or gift tax of an interest in property to a skip person. A skip person may be a natural person or certain trusts. All persons assigned to the second or more remote generation below the transferor are skip persons (*e.g.*, grandchildren and great-grandchildren). Trusts are skip persons if (1) all interests in the trust are held by skip persons, or (2) no person holds an interest in the trust and at no time after the transfer may a distribution (including distributions and terminations) be made to a non-skip person.

A taxable termination is a termination (by death, lapse of time, release of power, or otherwise) of an interest in property held in trust unless, immediately after such termination, a non-skip person has an interest in the property, or unless at no time after the termination may a distribution (including a distribution upon termination) be made from the trust to a skip person.

A taxable distribution is a distribution from a trust to a skip person (other than a taxable termination or direct skip). If a transferor allocates generation-skipping transfer tax exemption to a trust prior to the taxable distribution, generation-skipping transfer tax may be avoided.

The generation-skipping transfer tax is imposed using a flat rate equal to the highest estate tax rate (40 percent). Tax is imposed on cumulative generation-skipping transfers in excess of the generation-skipping transfer tax exemption amount in effect for the year of the transfer. The generation-skipping transfer tax exemption for a given year is equal to the estate tax exemption amount in effect for that year.

The generation-skipping exemption may be allocated by a transferor (or his or her executor) to transferred property, and in some situations it is automatically allocated. The allocation of generation-skipping transfer tax exemption effectively reduces the tax rate on a generation-skipping transfer.

The tax rate on generation-skipping transfers is a flat rate of tax equal to the maximum estate and gift tax rate (40 percent) multiplied by the "inclusion ratio." The inclusion ratio with respect to any property transferred indicates the amount of "generation-skipping transfer tax exemption" allocated to a trust (or to property transferred in a direct skip) relative to the total value of property transferred. If, for example, a taxpayer transfers $5 million in property to a trust and allocates $5 million of exemption to the transfer, the inclusion ratio is zero, and the applicable tax rate on any subsequent generation-skipping transfers from the trust is zero percent (40 percent multiplied by the inclusion ratio of zero). If, however, the taxpayer allocated only $2.5 million of exemption to the transfer, the inclusion ratio is 0.5, and the applicable tax rate on any subsequent generation-skipping transfers from the trust is 20 percent (40 percent multiplied by the inclusion ratio of 0.5). If the taxpayer allocates no exemption to the transfer, the inclusion ratio is one, and the applicable tax rate on any subsequent generation-skipping transfers from the trust is 40 percent (40 percent multiplied by the inclusion ratio of one).

The inclusion ratio is one minus the applicable fraction. The applicable fraction is the amount of exemption allocated to a trust (or to a direct skip) divided by the value of assets transferred.

Common Tax Rate Table. The gift and estate taxes are unified so that a single graduated rate schedule and effective exemption amount apply to an individual's cumulative taxable gifts and bequests. The unified estate and gift tax rates begin at 18 percent on the first $10,000 in cumulative taxable transfers and reach 40 percent on cumulative taxable transfers over $1,000,000. The new law effectively exempts approximately $11.2 million ($22.4 million for marrieds) in 2018 in cumulative taxable transfers from the GST or estate tax. Unused exemption as of the death of a spouse generally is available for use by the surviving spouse if the deceased spouse makes a portability election on a timely-filed estate tax return (Form 706).

Transfers between Spouses. A 100-percent marital deduction generally is permitted for the value of property transferred between spouses. In addition, transfers of "qualified terminable interest property" are eligible for the marital deduction. Qualified terminable interest property is property: (1) that passes from the decedent, (2) in which the surviving spouse has a "qualifying income interest for life," and (3) to which an election under these rules applies.

A qualifying income interest for life exists if: (1) the surviving spouse is entitled to all the income from the property (payable annually or at more frequent intervals) or has the right to use the property during the spouse's life, and (2) no person has the power to appoint any part of the property to any person other than the surviving spouse. A marital deduction generally is denied for property passing to a surviving spouse who is not a citizen of the United States.

A marital deduction is permitted, however, for property passing to a qualified domestic trust of which the noncitizen surviving spouse is a beneficiary. A qualified domestic trust is a trust that has as its trustee at least one U.S. citizen or U.S. corporation. No corpus may be distributed from a qualified domestic trust unless the U.S. trustee has the right to withhold any estate tax imposed on the distribution.

Transfers to Charity. Contributions to charitable organizations and certain other organizations may be deducted from the value of a gift or from the value of the assets in an estate for federal gift or estate tax purposes. The effect of the deduction generally is to remove the full fair market value of assets transferred to charity from the gift or estate tax base; unlike the income tax charitable deduction, there are no percentage limits on the deductible amount. For estate tax purposes, the charitable deduction is limited to the value of the transferred property that is required to be included in the gross estate. A charitable contribution of a partial interest in property, such as a remainder or future interest, generally is not deductible for gift or estate tax purposes.

Credits Against Tax. After accounting for allowable deductions, a gross amount of estate tax is computed. Estate tax liability is then determined by subtracting allowable credits from the gross estate tax.

Unified Credit. A unified credit is available with respect to taxable transfers by gift and at death. The unified credit offsets tax, is computed using the applicable estate and gift tax rates on a specified amount of transfers, and is referred to as the applicable exclusion amount, or exemption amount. In 2018, the inflation-indexed exemption amount is estimated to be $11.2 million.

Exemption used during life to offset taxable gifts reduces the amount of exemption that remains at death to offset the value of a decedent's estate. An election is available under which exemption that is not used by a decedent may be used by the decedent's surviving spouse (exemption portability).

Estate tax credits are also allowed for: (1) gift tax paid on certain pre-1977 gifts (before the estate and gift tax computations were integrated); (2) estate tax paid on certain prior transfers (to limit the estate tax burden when estate tax is imposed on transfers of the same property in two estates by reason of deaths in rapid succession); and (3) certain foreign death taxes paid (generally, where the property is situated in a foreign country but included in the decedent's U.S. gross estate).

Income Tax Basis in Property Received. Gain or loss on the disposition of property is measured by the taxpayer's amount realized or gross proceeds received on the disposition, less the taxpayer's basis in the property. Basis generally represents a taxpayer's investment in property with adjustments made to reflect, for example, capital improvements or depreciation.

When a taxpayer receives a gift or bequest of appreciated property, he or she does not realize income for tax purposes. Instead special rules determine the recipient's basis in the assets received depending on whether the property was transferred while the donor was still alive or after the donor died.

Basis in Property Received by Lifetime Gift. When property is received from a donor during the donor's lifetime, the gift generally takes a carryover basis which means that the basis in the hands of the donee is the same as it was in the hands of the donor. The basis of property transferred by lifetime gift is also increased, but not above fair market value, by any gift tax paid by the donor. The basis of a lifetime gift, however, generally cannot exceed the property's fair market value on the date of the gift. If a donor's basis in property is greater than the fair market value of the property on the date of the gift, then, for purposes of determining loss on a subsequent sale of the property, the donee's basis is the property's fair market value on the date of the gift.

Basis in Property Acquired from a Decedent. When property is acquired from a decedent's estate, the basis of the property will be stepped-up to the property's fair market value on the date of the decedent's death (or, if the alternate valuation date is elected, the earlier of six months after the decedent's death or the date the property is sold or distributed by the estate). Providing a fair market value basis eliminates the recognition of income on any appreciation of the property that occurred prior to the decedent's death and eliminates the tax benefit from any unrealized loss.

In community property states, a surviving spouse's one-half share of community property held by the decedent and the surviving spouse (under the community property laws of any state, U.S. possession, or foreign country) generally is treated as having passed from the decedent and, thus, is eligible for stepped-up basis. Thus, both the decedent's one-half share and the surviving spouse's one-half share are stepped up to fair market value.

This rule applies if at least one-half of the whole of the community interest is includible in the decedent's gross estate.

Stepped-up basis treatment generally is denied to certain interests in foreign entities. Stock in a passive foreign investment company (including those for which a mark-to-market election has been made) generally takes a carryover basis, except that stock of a passive foreign investment company for which a decedent-shareholder had made a qualified electing fund election is allowed a stepped-up basis. Stock owned by a decedent in a domestic international sales corporation (or former domestic international sales corporation) takes a stepped-up basis reduced by the amount (if any) which would have been included in gross income as a dividend if the decedent had lived and sold the stock at its fair market value on the estate tax valuation date which generally is the date of the decedent's death unless an alternate valuation date is elected.

§ 7.02 Effect of the Tax Cuts and Jobs Act on the Unified Credit for Federal Estate, Gift and GST Taxes

Under pre-Tax Cuts and Job Act law, the first $5 million (as adjusted for inflation in years after 2011) of transferred property was exempt from estate and gift tax. For estates of decedents dying and gifts made in 2018, this "basic exclusion amount" under pre-Tax Cuts and Jobs Act law was scheduled to adjust to $5.6 million ($11,200,000 for a married couple).

Estate and Gift Tax Exemption Doubled Under New Law. The Tax Cuts and Jobs Act doubled the estate and gift tax exemption amount from $5 million to $10 million ($20 million per married couple) for estates of decedents dying and gifts made after December 31, 2017 and before January 1, 2026. The $10 million amount, indexed for inflation occurring after 2011, is expected to be approximately $11.2 million in 2018 ($22.4 million per married couple). Therefore, a decedent who dies in 2018 can pass approximately $11.2 million of assets free of estate, gift or generation-skipping transfer tax to heirs. A married couple dying in 2018 can pass approximately $22.4 million to heirs free of any transfer taxes.

> **Planning Tip.** As a result of the vastly increased exemption amounts for estate and gift tax, everyone is encouraged to reevaluate their estate plans. And, although the Jobs Act does not specifically mention generation-skipping transfers, it can be assumed that the generation-skipping transfer tax exemption amount will also be increased in the same manner as the unified credit because the GST tax exemption amount is based on the basic exclusion amount for the estate tax which is doubled under the new law. And you are

also encouraged to consider whether there is any state estate tax exposure in your jurisdiction.

Additional Planning Tip. Because the doubling of the estate and gift tax exclusion amount will expire for decedents dying and gifts made after December 31, 2025, the next several years present a tremendous opportunity for wealthy individuals and married couples to make large gifts, including those that leverage the amount of the available exclusion, such as those to grantor retained annuity trusts (GRATs). Unless Congress takes action before then, for decedents dying and gifts made after 2025, the basic exclusion amount will revert to $5 million, as adjusted for inflation under the C-CPI-U because, unlike many other provisions in the 2017 Tax Cuts and Jobs Act, the provision governing the inflation adjustment is not subject to sunset.

GST Tax Exemption Amount. Although the Tax Cuts and Jobs Act does not specifically mention generation-skipping transfers, it can be assumed that the generation-skipping transfer tax exemption amount will also be increased in the same manner as the unified credit because the GST tax exemption amount is based on the basic exclusion amount which is doubled under the new law. Portability does not apply for purposes of the GST tax.

Basis Considerations. Because the Tax Cuts and Jobs Act did not specifically address basis considerations in the new law, the old law continues to apply. Therefore, heirs will continue to receive a "stepped-up date of death" basis for inherited assets for purposes of any subsequent sale. A stepped-up date of death basis eliminates any gain upon the subsequent sale of appreciated assets. The basis of assets transferred during the donor's lifetime will receive a carry-over basis in the recipient's hands.

Planning Tip. The doubling of the estate and gift tax exclusion amount will expire for decedents dying and gifts made after December 31, 2025. Therefore, for the next eight years, wealthy individuals have the opportunity to take advantage of the large gift tax exemption amount and make gifts to loved ones free of gift tax.

Additional Planning Tip. Heirs should be aware that they will continue to receive a "stepped-up, date of death" basis for inherited assets for purposes of any subsequent sale of these assets.

Income Tax Treatment of Income from Trusts and Estates. The Tax Cuts and Jobs Act replaced the old rate structure for income tax rates imposed on estates and trusts with the following updated rate structure:

Estate and Trusts for Tax Years Beginning in 2018

If taxable income is:		The tax is:	
Over—	but not over—		of the amount over—
$0	$2,550	10%	$0
2,550	9,150	$255 + 24%	2,550
9,150	12,500	1,839 + 35%	9,150
12,500		3,011.50 + 37%	12,500

Capital Gains Tax Rates Imposed on Estates and Trusts. In the case of an estate, or trust, any adjusted net capital gain that would otherwise be taxed at the 10 or 15% rate is taxed at 0%. Any adjusted net capital gain that would otherwise be taxed at rates over 15% but below 39.6% is taxed at a 15% rate. A 20% rate applies to any adjusted net capital gain received by taxpayers in the top 39.6% income tax bracket. The new law generally retains the prior-law maximum rates on net capital gain and qualified dividends. The breakpoints between the 0 and 15% rates ("15% breakpoint") and the 15 and 20% rates ("20% breakpoint") are the same amounts as the breakpoints under prior law, except the breakpoints are indexed using the C-CPI-U. Thus, for 2018, the 15% breakpoint is $2,600 for estates and trusts. The 20% breakpoint is $12,700 for estates and trusts.

Therefore, in the case of an estate or trust with adjusted net capital gain, to the extent the gain would not result in taxable income exceeding the 15% breakpoint, such gain is not taxed. Any adjusted net capital gain that would result in taxable income exceeding the 15% breakpoint but not exceeding the 20% breakpoint is taxed at 15%. The remaining adjusted net capital gain is taxed at 20%.

Unrecaptured gain is taxed at a maximum rate of 25%, and 28% rate gain is taxed at a maximum rate of 28%. Any amount of unrecaptured gain or 28% rate gain otherwise taxed at a 10 or 15% rate is taxed at the otherwise applicable rate.

In addition, a 3.8% tax is imposed on net investment income of an estate or trust. The net investment income of an estate or trust is computed by taking the lesser of (1) the undistributed net investment income, or (2) the excess (if any) of the estate or trust's adjusted gross income over the dollar amount at which the highest income tax bracket for estates and trusts begins for that year ($12,500 in 2018).

Reduction in Estate Tax Return Filings Predicted. According to the IRS Statistics of Income tables presenting estate tax return data for Filing Year 2016, a total of 5,219 taxable estate tax returns were filed contrasted with 7,192 nontaxable estate tax returns. Of the taxable returns, 2,402 fell within the $5 to $10 million gross estate range, 1,293 in the $10 to

$20 million range. Only 300 returns were filed with gross estates in excess of $50 million. These statistics primarily reflect data from the estates of decedents who died in 2015, when the basic exclusion amount was $5.43 million, but also include some returns for decedents who died in years prior to 2015, as well as a small number of estates with respect to deaths that occurred in 2016. The large increase in the basic exclusion amount after 2017 is expected to lead to further decreases in the number of taxable estates.

CHAPTER 8

Alternative Minimum Tax (AMT)

§ 8.01 What is the AMT and How is it Calculated?
§ 8.02 What is the Effect of the Tax Cuts and Jobs Act on the AMT?

§ 8.01 What is the AMT and How is it Calculated?

Special income tax breaks are available under the tax laws for certain kinds of income and expenses. Taxpayers who take advantage of these tax breaks may reduce their regular income tax but may also expose themselves to the alternative minimum tax (AMT). The AMT is an alternate taxing system that is imposed on an individual, estate, or trust in an amount by which the taxpayer's "tentative minimum tax" exceeds the taxpayer's regular income tax for the tax year. The AMT is a tax that is in addition to, not instead of, the regular tax imposed on a taxpayer's income. Individuals must use Form 6251, *Alternative Minimum Tax—Individuals*, to compute their AMT liability.

The AMT originally directed at wealthy taxpayers who offset taxable income through the clever use of deductions, exemptions and credits that receive preferential treatment under the tax laws. The AMT was created to make sure that these resourceful taxpayers, who legitimately arrange their affairs to minimize their tax liability, pay their fair share of tax. As a result, the AMT includes in its taxable base many of the items that the regular tax system allows taxpayers to exclude.

So-called adjustments and preference items that are afforded favorable treatment under the regular income tax rules are eliminated for AMT purposes. This results in a broadened tax base that is subject to AMT rates that are lower than the top regular income tax rates.

The AMT tax is imposed against individuals (including nonresident aliens), estates, trusts, and corporations (including foreign corporations engaged in a U.S. trade or business). However, note that the Tax Cuts and Jobs Act eliminates the corporate AMT. A two-tiered, graduated rate schedule is applicable to noncorporate taxpayers. The lower tier consists of a 26 percent tax rate and the upper tier consists of a 28 percent tax rate.

For 2017 taxes (and prior to the changes made by the Act), the tentative minimum tax is the sum of:

1. 26% of so much of the taxable excess as does not exceed $187,800 ($93,900 in the case of a married individual filing a separate return); and
2. 28% of the remaining taxable excess.

The breakpoints are indexed for inflation.

An individual's AMT liability is calculated as follows:

1. Start with taxpayer's taxable income from Form 1040.
2. Add or subtract certain adjustments.
3. Add all tax preference items (described in more detail below).
4. The sum is the alternative minimum taxable income (AMTI), which is often characterized as the heart of the AMT.
5. Subtract the applicable exemption amount, if any. This equals the alternative minimum tax base (AMTB).
6. Multiply the AMTB by the alternative minimum tax rates (26% of the first $187,800 of AMTB in 2017 plus 28% of the excess of AMTB over $187,800). This will result in the tentative minimum tax. If this figure exceeds the taxpayer's regular income tax bill, the taxpayer owes AMT.
7. Subtract the regular tax liability.
8. This is the AMT that must be paid in addition to the regular tax. The result of this computation is that the taxpayer pays the higher of the tentative minimum tax or the tax liability on taxable income computed on Form 1040 without consideration of the AMT.

Tax Preferences. When taxpayers compute AMT liability, the critical component is determining alternative minimum taxable income (AMTI). Again, this is the taxpayer's taxable income increased by certain preference items and adjusted by determining the tax treatment of certain items in a manner that negates the deferral of income resulting from the regular tax treatment of those items.

Taxpayers subject to the AMT, must add back tax preference items to their taxable income when computing AMTI for AMT purposes. Preferences can take the form of deductions, lower tax rates, or exclusions that generate tax savings for the taxpayer under the regular taxing system. Generally, only the amount of the benefit received, less the benefit otherwise allowed, is counted as a tax preference item. The tax preference items are discussed below:

1. **Depletion.** Taxpayers must refigure depletion deductions for purposes of the AMTI computation.

2. **Intangible Drilling Costs.** In calculating AMTI, a taxpayer must add to taxable income a tax preference equal to the excess intangible drilling costs, over 65% of the income from the properties. The tax preference for excess intangible drilling costs does not apply to independent oil and gas producers.

3. **Tax-Exempt Interest from Private Activity Bonds**. When computing AMTI, add back tax-exempt interest on specified private activity bonds, which means any private bond issued after August 7, 1986, where the interest is tax exempt. The following types of tax-exempt housing bonds, if issued after July 30, 2008, are not treated as private activity bonds for AMT purposes. Therefore, interest generated by these housing bonds will not be subject to the AMT and will not be an AMT tax preference item that must be added to the taxpayer's regular taxable income base in computing the taxpayer's AMTI:
   — An exempt facility bond if it is part of an issue, 95% or more of the net proceeds of which are to be used to provide qualified residential rental projects;
   — A qualified mortgage bond; and
   — A qualified veterans' mortgage bond.

4. **Accelerated Depreciation of Property Acquired Before 1987.** If a taxpayer acquired real property before 1987, the difference between the depreciation that would have been allowable if the straight-line method had been used and the accelerated depreciation claimed for regular tax purposes is considered a tax preference item. As a result, when computing AMTI, the taxpayer must use the straight-line method to figure depreciation on real property even if for regular tax purposes he or she had used accelerated depreciation using pre-1987 rules.

5. **Exclusion for Gains on Sale of Small Business Stock.** If certain conditions are met, noncorporate investors may exclude some or all of the gain realized on the sale or exchange of small business stock held for more than five years. Generally, a percentage of the excluded gain is classified as a tax preference item when computing an investor's AMTI. Seven percent of the investor's total realized gain for the sale or exchange of small business stock will be treated as a preference item for AMT purposes.

Adjustments Taken into Consideration When Computing AMTI. Individuals must make the following adjustments when computing AMTI:

1. **Depreciation.** In calculating AMTI, a taxpayer may not deduct depreciation for personal property under the modified accelerated cost recovery system (MACRS).

2. **Mining Exploration and Development Costs.** Mining exploration and development costs are capitalized and amortized over a ten-year period.

3. **Certain Long-Term Contracts.** Taxable income from a long-term contract (other than a home construction contract) is computed using the percentage of completion method of accounting. This requirement applies even though the taxpayer may otherwise be exempt from using the percentage of completion method for regular tax purposes.

4. **Pollution Control Facilities.** In calculating AMTI, a taxpayer must use the straight-line method of cost recovery for any pollution control facilities. The adjustment to taxable income in calculating AMTI will be a positive adjustment when the deduction for AMT purposes is less than the deduction for regular tax purposes.

5. **Itemized Deductions.** In calculating AMTI, a taxpayer must make the following adjustments:
   - State, local, and foreign real property taxes may not be deducted.
   - Deductions for state and local personal property taxes are not allowed.
   - Deductions for state, local, and foreign income, war profits, and excess profits taxes are not allowed.
   - State and local sales tax deductions are not allowed.
   - Deductions for medical expenses are allowed only to the extent they exceed 10% of the taxpayer's adjusted gross income.
   - Generally, a taxpayer may not deduct interest on a home equity loan in calculating AMTI. However, a taxpayer may deduct the interest on a home equity loan if he or she uses the proceeds of the loan to make a substantial improvement to the principal residence or to acquire or construct another qualified residence. Interest on loans used for business purposes is deductible in calculating taxable income and in calculating AMTI.
   - A taxpayer may deduct the interest on loans used to acquire private activity bonds as investment interest because a taxpayer must include the interest on such bonds in calculating AMTI.
   - Interest deducted on Schedule C, *Profit or Loss from Business* and Schedule F, *Profit or Loss from Farming* is not an adjustment in calculating AMTI.
   - The phase-out for itemized deductions other than medical expenses, investment interest, and casualty and theft losses for regular tax purposes does not apply in calculating AMTI.
   - Miscellaneous itemized deductions reported on Schedule A are not allowed when calculating the AMT. Therefore, miscellaneous deductions must be added back when computing AMTI and are reflected as a positive adjustment on Form 6251.

6. **Standard Deduction/Exemptions**. A taxpayer may not deduct the standard deduction or personal and dependency exemptions when calculating AMTI.

7. **Research and Experimental Expenditures.** The amount allowable as a deduction for research and experimentation expenditures from passive activities is capitalized and amortized over a ten-year period.
8. **Incentive Stock Options.** The regular tax rules relating to incentive stock options do not apply. The taxpayer must include the difference between the fair market value (FMV) of the stock and any amount the taxpayer paid for it in calculating AMTI in the year the taxpayer's rights to the stock are not forfeitable.
9. **Passive Activity Losses.** In calculating AMTI, a taxpayer may not deduct passive activity losses.
10. **Passive Farming Activities.** An individual may not deduct a loss from a tax shelter farming activity in calculating AMTI. The tax shelter farm activity loss takes into account the adjustments and tax preference items used in calculating AMTI. The taxpayer may deduct a loss from a tax shelter farm activity as a deduction of the activity in the next tax year. A tax shelter farming activity includes any farming activity that is a farming syndicate or that is a passive activity.
11. **Net Operating Loss Deduction.** In calculating AMTI, a taxpayer may not deduct the net operating loss allowed for regular tax purposes.
12. **Publicly Traded Partnership (PTP).** If a taxpayer had losses from a PTP, the taxpayer will have to refigure the loss using any AMT adjustments and preferences and any AMT prior year disallowed loss.
13. **Circulation Expenses.** Noncorporate taxpayers who deduct circulation expenditures (*i.e.*, the costs of establishing, maintaining, or increasing the circulation of a newspaper, magazine, or other periodical) from regular taxable income by expensing them must compute AMTI as if the expenditures were capitalized and ratably amortized over a three-year period. If the expenditures create a tax loss for the taxpayer, all unrecovered expenditures may be claimed against AMTI. Recomputed deductions must also be reflected in the amount of gain or loss included in AMTI. If property for which deductions have been recomputed is sold, the adjusted basis of the property must be based on adjusted circulation deductions rather than the deductions used to calculate regular taxable income.
14. **Domestic Production Activities Deduction.** The domestic production activities deduction is allowed for both individuals and corporations against the AMT. For individuals, the calculation of the deduction is the same for both regular income tax and AMT liability.

AMT Exemption. Under pre-Tax Cuts and Jobs Act law, for 2017, the AMT exemption amounts were scheduled to be:

- $84,500 for marrieds filing jointly/surviving spouses;
- $54,300 for other unmarried individuals;
- 50% of the marrieds-filing-jointly amount for marrieds filing separately, *i.e.,* $42,250.

And, those exemption amounts were reduced by an amount equal to 25% of the amount by which the individual's AMTI exceeded:

- $160,900 for marrieds filing jointly and surviving spouses (phase-out complete at $498,900);
- $120,700 for unmarried individuals (phase-out completed at $337,900); and
- 50-percent of the marrieds-filing-jointly amount for marrieds filing separately, *i.e.,* $80,450 (phase-out completed at $249,450).

§ 8.02 What is the Effect of the Tax Cuts and Jobs Act on the AMT?

The Tax Cuts and Jobs Act increases the AMT exemption amounts for individuals effective January 1, 2018 and before January 1, 2026. For 2018, these amounts are as follows:

- For joint returns and surviving spouses, $109,400.
- For single taxpayers, $70,300.
- For marrieds filing separately, $54,700.

These exemption amounts are reduced (not below zero) to an amount equal to 25% of the amount by which the AMTI of the taxpayer exceeds the phase-out amounts, increased as follows:

- For joint returns and surviving spouses, $1 million.
- For all other taxpayers (other than estates and trusts), $500,000.

The AMT exemptions for individuals will completely phase out in 2018 at AMTI of:

- $1,437,600 for marrieds filing jointly/surviving spouses ($1,000,000 + $437,600 [4 × $109,400]);
- $781,200 for other unmarried taxpayers ($500,000 + $281,200 [4 × $70,300]); and
- $718,800 for marrieds filing separately ($500,000 + $218,800 [4 × $54,700]).

All of the increased amounts are adjusted annually for inflation.

Practical Tip: The higher 2018 AMT exemption may mean that you won't be subject to the AMT in 2018.

CHAPTER 9

Pass-Through Entities

§ 9.01 New 20% Deduction for Pass-Through Business Income

Under pre-Tax Cuts and Jobs Act law, the net income of pass-through businesses such as sole proprietorships, partnerships, limited liability companies (LLCs), and S corporations was not subject to an entity-level tax and income was, instead, reported by the owners or shareholders on their individual income tax returns. Thus, the income was effectively subject to individual income tax rates.

The Tax Cuts and Jobs Act adds a new 20% deduction for tax years beginning after December 31, 2017 and before January 1, 2026. A new section to the Internal Revenue Code provides that a non-corporate taxpayer, including a trust or estate, who has qualified business income (QBI) from a partnership, S corporation, or sole proprietorship may deduct:

1. The lesser of: (a) the "combined qualified business income amount" of the taxpayer, or (b) 20% of the excess, if any, of the taxable income of the taxpayer for the tax year over the sum of net capital gain and the aggregate amount of the qualified cooperative dividends of the taxpayer for the tax year; plus
2. The lesser of: (i) 20% of the aggregate amount of the qualified cooperative dividends of the taxpayer for the tax year, or (ii) taxable income (reduced by the net capital gain) of the taxpayer for the tax year.

The term "combined qualified business income amount" means, for any tax year, an amount equal to: (i) the deductible amount for each qualified trade or business of the taxpayer (defined as 20% of the taxpayer's QBI subject to a W-2 wage/qualified property limitation; *plus* (ii) 20% of the aggregate amount of qualified real estate investment trust (REIT) dividends and qualified publicly traded partnership income of the taxpayer for the tax year.

The term "QBI" is generally defined as the net amount of "qualified items of income, gain, deduction, and loss" relating to any qualified trade or business of the taxpayer. The term "qualified items of income, gain, deduction, and loss" is defined as items of income, gain, deduction, and loss to the extent these items are effectively connected with the conduct of a trade or business within the U.S. and included or allowed in determining taxable income for the year. If the net amount of qualified income, gain, deduction, and loss relating to qualified trade or businesses of the taxpayer for any tax year is less than zero, the amount is treated as a loss from a qualified trade or business in the succeeding tax year.

The term "QBI" does *not* include: (1) certain investment items; (2) reasonable compensation paid to the taxpayer by any qualified trade or business for services rendered with respect to the trade or business; (3) any guaranteed payment to a partner for services rendered with respect to the trade or business; or (4) a payment to a partner under Code Sec. 707(a) for services rendered with respect to the trade or business.

> **Comment.** This new deduction allows taxpayers to deduct a portion of their "taxable income" if it is less than a portion of their relevant business income. It cannot be claimed if the taxpayer has no relevant business income.
>
> The qualified property component means that a taxpayer might be able to claim this deduction if the taxpayer carries on a qualified trade or business that has few or no employees but generates income using its depreciable tangible assets.

Limitations. A qualified trade or business's deductible amount generally is the greater of:

1. 50% of the W-2 wages with respect to the qualified trade or business, or
2. The sum of 25% of the W-2 wages paid with respect to the qualified trade or business *plus* 2.5% of the unadjusted basis, immediately after acquisition, of all "qualified property." Qualified property is defined as

meaning tangible, depreciable property which is held by and available for use in the qualified trade or business at the close of the tax year, which is used at any point during the tax year in the production of qualified business income, and the depreciable period of which has not ended before the close of the tax year.

For a partnership or S corporation, each partner or shareholder is treated as having W-2 wages and unadjusted basis for the tax year in an amount equal to his or her allocable share of the W-2 wages and unadjusted basis of the entity for the tax year. A partner's or shareholder's allocable share of W-2 wages is determined in the same way as the partner's or shareholder's allocable share of wage expenses. A partner's or shareholder's allocable share of the unadjusted basis of qualified property is determined in the same manner as the partner's or shareholder's allocable share of depreciation. For an S corporation, an allocable share is the shareholder's pro rata share of an item. However, the W-2 wages/qualified property limit does not apply if the taxpayer's taxable income for the tax year is equal to or less than $315,000 for married individuals filing jointly ($157,500 for other individuals). The application of the W-2 wage/qualified property limit is phased in for individuals with taxable income exceeding these thresholds over the next $100,000 of taxable income for married individuals filing jointly ($50,000 for other individuals). The threshold amounts are adjusted for inflation for tax years beginning after 2018.

Thresholds and Exclusions. The deduction for pass-through income is also available to specified agricultural or horticultural cooperatives, in an amount equal to the lesser of (i) 20% of the excess of the co-op's gross income over any qualified cooperative dividends paid during the tax year for the tax year, or (ii) the greater of (a) 50% of the W-2 wages of the co-op with respect to its trade or business, or (b) the sum of 25% of the W-2 wages of the cooperative with respect to its trade or business plus 2.5% of the unadjusted basis immediately after acquisition of qualified property of the cooperative.

The deduction is taken "below the line," which means that it reduces the taxpayer's taxable income but not adjusted gross income. But it is available regardless of whether taxpayers itemize deductions or take the standard deduction. In general, the deduction cannot exceed 20% of the excess of the taxpayer's taxable income over net capital gain. If QBI is less than zero it is treated as a loss from a qualified business in the following year.

Rules are in place to deter high-income taxpayers from attempting to convert wages or other compensation for personal services into income eligible for the deduction. For taxpayers with taxable income above $157,500 ($315,000 for joint filers), an exclusion from QBI of income from "specified service" trades or businesses is phased in. These are trades or businesses involving the performance of services in the fields of health, law, consulting, athletics, financial or brokerage services, or where the principal asset is the reputation or skill of one or more employees or owners. Here's how the phase-in works:

1. If taxable income is at least $50,000 above the threshold, *i.e.*, $207,500 ($157,500 + $50,000), all of the net income from the specified service trade or business is excluded from QBI. (Joint filers would use an amount $100,000 above the $315,000 threshold, viz., $415,000.)
2. If your taxable income is between $157,500 and $207,500, you would exclude only that percentage of income derived from a fraction the numerator of which is the excess of taxable income over $157,500 and the denominator of which is $50,000. So, for example, if taxable income is $167,500 ($10,000 above $157,500), only 20% of the specified service income would be excluded from QBI ($10,000/$50,000). (For joint filers, the same operation would apply using the $315,000 threshold, and a $100,000 phase-out range.)

Additionally, for taxpayers with taxable income more than the above thresholds, a limitation on the amount of the deduction is phased in based either on wages paid or wages paid plus a capital element. Here's how it works: If taxable income is at least $50,000 above the threshold, the taxpayer's deduction for QBI cannot exceed the greater of (1) 50% of the taxpayer's allocable share of the W-2 wages paid with respect to the qualified trade or business, or (2) the sum of 25% of such wages plus 2.5% of the unadjusted basis immediately after acquisition of tangible depreciable property used in the business (including real estate).

If the taxpayer's QBI were $100,000, leading to a deduction of $20,000 (20% of $100,000), but the greater of (1) or (2) above were only $16,000, the taxpayer's deduction would be limited to $16,000. If the taxpayer's taxable income were between $157,500 and $207,500, the taxpayer would only incur a percentage of the $4,000 reduction, with the percentage worked out via the fraction discussed in the preceding paragraph. (For joint filers, the same operations would apply using the $315,000 threshold, and a $100,000 phase-out range.)

Other limitations may apply in certain circumstances, *e.g.,* for taxpayers with qualified cooperative dividends, qualified real estate investment trust (REIT) dividends, or income from publicly-traded partnerships.

Practical Tip. Trades or businesses that ARE specified service trades or businesses and thus do not qualify for the deduction, include services in the fields of accounting, actuarial science, athletics, brokerage services, consulting, financial services, health, law, or the performing arts, as well as services consisting of investing and investment management, trading, or dealing in securities, partnership interests, or commodities, or a service trade or business whose principal asset is the reputation or skill of one or more of its employees or owners. Note, however, that a taxpayer carrying on a specified service trade or business can claim a modified qualified business deduction if his or her taxable income for the tax year is less than $415,000 for taxpayers filing a joint return or $207,500 for all other taxpayers.

Note that architecture and engineering are not specified service trades or businesses, and so can be qualified trades or businesses under this provision if they otherwise qualify. Further, for guidance on the types of activities that qualify as services in the fields of health, the performing arts, and consulting, you may want to refer to the rules determining whether a qualified personal service corporation may use the cash method of accounting.

§ 9.02 Carried Interests—Partnership Interests

In general, the receipt of a capital interest for services provided results in taxable compensation for the service provider. However, under a safe harbor rule, the receipt of a profits interest in exchange for services provided is not a taxable event to the recipient if the profits interest entitles the holder to share only in gains and profits generated after the date of issuance (and certain other requirements are met).

Typically, private equity and hedge fund managers guide the investment strategy and act as general partners to an investment partnership, while outside investors act as limited partners. Fund managers are compensated in two ways. First, to the extent that they invest their own capital in the funds, they share in the appreciation of fund assets. Second, they charge the outside investors two kinds of annual "performance" fees: a percentage of total fund assets, typically 2%, and a percentage of the fund's earnings, typically 20%. The 20% profits interest is often carried over from year to year until a cash payment is made, usually following the closing out of an investment.

This type of payment is called a "carried interest."

Under pre-Act law, carried interests were taxed in the hands of the taxpayer (*i.e.*, the fund manager) at favorable capital gain rates instead of as ordinary income.

For tax years beginning after December 31, 2017, the new law effectively imposes a three-year holding period requirement in order for certain partnership interests received in connection with the performance of services to be taxed as long-term capital gain. If the three-year holding period is not met with respect to an applicable partnership interest held by the taxpayer, the taxpayer's gain will be treated as a short-term gain and taxed at ordinary income rates.

§ 9.03 Substantial Built-In Loss on Transfer of Partnership Interests

In general, a partnership does not adjust the basis of partnership property following the transfer of a partnership interest unless either the partnership has made a one-time election to make basis adjustments, or the partnership has a substantial built-in loss immediately after the transfer. If an election is in effect, or if the partnership has a substantial built-in loss immediately after the transfer, adjustments are made with respect to the transferee-partner. These adjustments are to account for the difference between the transferee-partner's proportionate share of the adjusted basis of the partnership property and the transferee's basis in his or her partnership interest.

Under pre-Act law, a substantial built-in loss exists if the partnership's adjusted basis in its property exceeds by more than $250,000 the fair market value of the partnership property. Certain securitization partnerships and electing investment partnerships are not treated as having a substantial built-in loss in certain instances and thus are not required to make basis adjustments to partnership property. For electing investment partnerships, in lieu of the partnership basis adjustments, a partner-level loss limitation rule applies.

For transfers of partnership interests after December 31, 2017, the definition of a substantial built-in loss is modified, affecting transfers of partnership interests. In addition to the present-law definition, a substantial built-in loss also exists if the transferee would be allocated a net loss in excess of $250,000 upon a hypothetical disposition by the partnership of all of the partnership's assets in a fully taxable transaction for cash equal to the assets' fair market value, immediately after the transfer of the partnership interest.

§ 9.04 Basis Limitation on Partner Losses from Partnership

In general, the passive loss rules limit deductions and credits from passive trade or business activities. The passive loss rules apply to individuals, estates and trusts, and closely-held corporations. A passive activity for this purpose is a trade or business activity in which the taxpayer owns an interest but does not materially participate. "Material participation" means that the taxpayer is involved in the operation of the activity on a basis that is regular, continuous, and substantial. Deductions attributable to passive activities, to the extent they exceed income from passive activities, generally may not be deducted against other income and are carried forward and treated as deductions and credits from passive activities in the next year.

Under pre-Act law, a limitation on excess farm losses applies to taxpayers other than C corporations. If a taxpayer other than a C corporation receives an applicable subsidy for the tax year, the amount of the "excess farm loss" is not allowed for the tax year, and is carried forward and treated as a deduction attributable to farming businesses in the next tax year. An excess farm loss for a tax year means the excess of aggregate deductions that are attributable to farming businesses over the sum of aggregate gross income or gain attributable to farming businesses plus the threshold amount. The threshold amount is the greater of (1) $300,000 ($150,000 for married individuals filing separately), or (2) for the 5-consecutive-year period preceding the tax year, the excess of the aggregate gross income or gain attributable to the taxpayer's farming businesses over the aggregate deductions attributable to the taxpayer's farming businesses.

For tax years beginning after December 31, 2017 and before January 1, 2026, the Act provides that the excess farm loss limitation doesn't apply, and instead a noncorporate taxpayer's "excess business loss" is disallowed.

Under the new rule, excess business losses are not allowed for the tax year but are instead carried forward and treated as part of the taxpayer's net operating loss (NOL) carryforward in subsequent tax years. This limitation applies *after* the application of the passive loss rules described above.

An excess business loss for the tax year is the excess of aggregate deductions of the taxpayer attributable to the taxpayer's trades and businesses, over the sum of aggregate gross income or gain of the taxpayer plus a threshold amount. The threshold amount for a tax year is $500,000 for married individuals filing jointly, and $250,000 for other individuals, with both amounts indexed for inflation.

In the case of a partnership or S corporation, the provision applies at the partner or shareholder level. Each partner's or S corporation shareholder's share of items of income, gain, deduction, or loss of the partnership or

S corporation is taken into account in applying the above limitation for the tax year of the partner or S corporation shareholder; and regulatory authority is provided to apply the new provision to any other pass-through entity to the extent necessary, as well as to require any additional reporting as the IRS determines is appropriate to carry out the purposes of the provision.

§ 9.05 Gain or Loss from Sale of Interest in Foreign Partnership

Gain or loss from the sale or exchange of a partnership interest generally is treated as gain or loss from the sale or exchange of a capital asset. However, the amount of money and the fair market value of property received in the exchange that represents the partner's share of certain ordinary income-producing assets of the partnership give rise to ordinary income rather than capital gain.

A foreign person that is engaged in a trade or business in the United States is taxed on income that is "effectively connected" with the conduct of that trade or business (*i.e.,* effectively connected gain or loss). Partners in a partnership are treated as engaged in the conduct of a trade or business within the United States if the partnership is so engaged.

In one example, in determining the source of gain or loss from the sale or exchange of an interest in a foreign partnership, the IRS applied an asset-use test and business activities test at the partnership level to determine the extent to which income derived from the sale or exchange was effectively connected with that U.S. business. However, a Tax Court case has instead held that, generally, gain or loss on sale or exchange by a foreign person of an interest in a partnership that is engaged in a U.S. trade or business is foreign-source.

For sales and exchanges on or after November 27, 2017, gain or loss from the sale or exchange of a partnership interest is effectively connected with a U.S. trade or business to the extent that the transferor would have had effectively connected gain or loss had the partnership sold all of its assets at fair market value as of the date of the sale or exchange. Any gain or loss from the hypothetical asset sale by the partnership must be allocated to interests in the partnership in the same manner as non-separately stated income and loss.

For sales, exchanges, and dispositions after December 31, 2017, the transferee of a partnership interest must withhold 10% of the amount realized on the sale or exchange of a partnership interest unless the transferor certifies that the transferor is not a nonresident alien individual or foreign corporation.

§ 9.06 Technical Termination of Partnerships

If a partnership terminates, its tax year closes for all partners. A partnership terminates if (1) its partners no longer carry on the partnership's business in partnership form; or (2) there is a sale or exchange of 50% or more of the total interests in partnership profits and capital within a 12-month period. This is described as a technical termination. There may be a "winding-up period" after the partners agree to dissolve the firm.

A partnership will not terminate when there is a change in business purpose. For example, a partnership does not terminate when it changes from developing property to holding property for investment purposes. In addition, the gift, bequest, inheritance, or liquidation of a partnership interest is not a sale or exchange for termination purposes. Thus, 50% or more of the partnership's assets may be distributed in liquidation of a partner's interest without terminating the partnership. But a contribution of property to a partnership, followed shortly by a distribution, may constitute a sale or exchange.

The partnership business is not considered to end on the death of one member of a two-man partnership, if the deceased partner's estate or successor continues to share in the profits and losses of the partnership.

If a partnership is terminated by a sale or exchange of an interest, the following is deemed to occur: The partnership contributes all of its assets and liabilities to a new partnership in exchange for an interest in the new partnership and, immediately thereafter, the terminated partnership distributes interests in the new partnership to the purchasing partner and the other remaining partners in proportion to their respective interests in the terminated partnership in liquidation of the terminated partnership, either for the continuation of the business by the new partnership or for its dissolution and winding up.

The capital accounts of the partners in the old partnership will carry over intact into the new partnership. In addition, the deemed contribution of assets and liabilities by the old partnership to the new partnership will be disregarded in determining the capital accounts in the new partnership.

The new partnership will retain the taxpayer identification number (TIN) of the old partnership, unless it has already applied for and obtained a new TIN.

The purchaser of an appreciated partnership interest will need to be sure the partnership has (or will make) an *optional adjustment to basis* election so that the purchaser can get a step-up for the purchaser's share of the basis of property inside the partnership.

Under a "technical termination," a partnership is considered as terminated if, within any 12-month period, there is a sale or exchange of 50% or more of the total interest in partnership capital and profits. A technical termination gives rise to a deemed contribution of all of the partnership's assets and liabilities to a new partnership in exchange for an interest in the new partnership, followed by a deemed distribution of interests in the new partnership to the purchasing partners and the other remaining partners. As a result of a technical termination, some of the tax attributes of the old partnership terminate: the partnership's tax year closes; partnership-level elections generally cease to apply; and the partnership depreciation recovery periods restart.

For partnership tax years beginning after December 31, 2017, the rule providing for the technical termination of a partnership is repealed. The repeal doesn't change the pre-Act law rule that a partnership is considered as terminated if no part of any business, financial operation, or venture of the partnership continues to be carried on by any of its partners in a partnership.

> **Planning Tip.** The elimination of the technical termination rules frees up members in a partnership to transfer interests in a partnership. This can be a beneficial part of estate and retirement planning, as a partner in a two-person partnership looking to "get out of the business" does not have to worry about destroying the business by transferring the partnership interest to a new member.

§ 9.07 Qualified Beneficiary of Electing Small Business Trust (ESBT)

An electing small business trust (ESBT) may be a shareholder of an S corporation. An ESBT is subject to income tax at the highest individual income tax rate on the portion of the trust which consists of stock in one or more S corporations ("S portion").

To qualify as an ESBT, all beneficiaries of the ESBT must be individuals, estates, charitable organizations, or a state or local government. A beneficiary that is a state or local government must hold a contingent interest in the trust and must not be a potential current beneficiary. Interests in qualifying trusts must be acquired by reason of gift, bequest, or other non-purchase acquisition. For a small business trust to be an eligible S corporation shareholder, no interest in the trust may be acquired by "purchase" (*i.e.,* acquired with a cost basis).

The income from the S portion of an ESBT is not included in the beneficiaries' income. The only items of income, loss, or deduction taken into account in computing the taxable income of the S portion of an ESBT are: (1) the items of income, loss, or deduction allocated to it as an S corporation shareholder under the rules of subchapter S, (2) gain or loss from the sale of the S corporation stock, and (3) to the extent provided in regulations, any state or local income taxes and administrative expenses of the ESBT are properly allocable to the S corporation stock. An ESBT can deduct interest on debt incurred to acquire S corporation stock when computing the taxable income of the S portion of the ESBT. Under pre-Act law, a nonresident alien individual may not be a shareholder of an S corporation and may not be a potential current beneficiary of an ESBT.

Effective on January 1, 2018, the Act allows a nonresident alien individual to be a potential current beneficiary of an ESBT.

§ 9.08 Charitable Contribution of Electing Small Business Trust (ESBT)

The deduction for charitable contributions applicable to trusts, rather than the deduction applicable to individuals, applies to an ESBT. Generally, a trust is allowed a charitable contribution deduction for amounts of gross income, without limitation, which pursuant to the terms of the governing instrument are paid for a charitable purpose. No carryover of excess contributions is allowed. An individual is allowed a charitable contribution deduction limited to certain percentages of adjusted gross income, generally with a five-year carryforward of amounts in excess of this limitation.

For tax years beginning after December 31, 2017, the new law provides that the charitable contribution deduction of an ESBT is not determined by the rules generally applicable to trusts but rather by the rules applicable to individuals. Thus, the percentage limitations and carryforward provisions applicable to individuals apply to charitable contributions made by the portion of an ESBT holding S corporation stock.

§ 9.09 S Corporation Conversions to C Corporation

After a termination of S corporation status, a shareholder can carry over losses that were disallowed because of the basis limitation and the at-risk limitation, to the post-termination transition period (PTTP) and may deduct these losses if there was sufficient basis (or at-risk amount) as of the last day of the PTTP. In addition, cash distributions by a former S corporation during the PTTP are treated as nontaxable distributions out of the S corporation's accumulated adjustments account (AAA), rather than as normal C corporation distributions.

The PTTP is:

1. The period beginning on the day after the last day of the corporation's last tax year as an S corporation and ending on the later of (a) the day that is one year after that day, or (b) the due date for filing the return for the corporation's last tax year as an S corporation (including extensions);
2. The 120-day period beginning on the date of any determination with respect to an audit of the taxpayer that follows the termination of the corporation's election and that adjusts a Subchapter S income, loss or deduction item that arises during the S corporation period (*i.e.*, the most recent continuous period during which the corporation was an S corporation); and
3. The 120-day period beginning on the date of a determination that the corporation's S election had terminated for an earlier year.

For distributions after December 22, 2017, distributions from an "eligible terminated S corporation" are treated as paid from its accumulated adjustments account and from its earnings and profits on a pro rata basis. Resulting adjustments are taken into account ratably over a six-year period. An eligible terminated S corporation is any C corporation which (i) was an S corporation on the date before the enactment date, (ii) revoked its S corporation election during the two-year period beginning on the enactment date, and (iii) had the same owners on the enactment date and on the revocation date (in the same proportion).

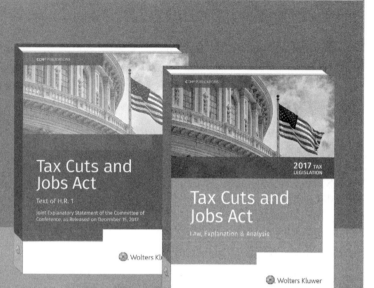